VIRTUAL REALITY PLAYHOUSE

by Nicholas Lavroff

WAITE GROUP
PRESS™

Corte Madera, California

Editorial Director • Scott Calamar
Development Editor • Mitchell Waite
Content Editors • Mitchell Waite, Heidi Brumbaugh
Production Manager • Julianne Ososke
Design and Production • Barbara Gelfand
Cover Design • Michael Rogondino
Computer Illustrations • Steven Epstein, John Hersey

Published by Waite Group Press, A Division of The Waite Group, Inc.
200 Tamal Plaza, Corte Madera, CA 94925. (415) 925-2575

Waite Group Press is distributed to bookstores and book wholesalers by Publishers Group West, Box 8843, Emeryville, CA 94662, 1-800-788-3123 (in California 510-658-3453).

Printed in the United States of America

92 93 94 • 10 9 8 7 6 5 4 3 2

Lavroff, Nicholas.
    Virtual Reality Playhouse / by Nicholas Lavroff.
        p. cm.
    Includes index.
    ISBN 1-878739-19-0: $22.95
    1. Human-computer interaction. 2. Virtual Reality I. Title
QA76.9.H85L39 1992
006--dc20   92-11273
                                                                CIP

Acknowledgments

We wish to acknowledge the following individuals and organizations for their kind assistance in the development of this book:

John Swenson (Power Glove and LCD Shutter Glasses code and instructions)

Lenny Lipton, Lhary Meyer, and Robert Akka of StereoGraphics Corp.

AJ Redmer and Spectrum HoloByte

Bill Freund and Horizon Entertainment

Caryn Mical and DoMark for permission to include MiG-29 and Lemme Out of Here!

Matthias Grabiak for permission to include Wire 3D

Oscar Garcia for permission to include 3DV

Justin Acklin (for the solution to Lemme Out of Here!)

Tom Baccei (or NE Body and NE Thing)and Michael Bielinski of Micro Synectic for permission to include the Stare-EO demo

Charles Cook and the University of California at Berkeley

Ian Andrews for permission to include the Superscape demo

George Coates' Performance Works

Special thanks to Lenny Lipton for permission to reproduce figures from his books *Stereoscopic Cinema* and *CrystalEyes*.

The Fine Print

All terms mentioned in this book that are known to be trademarks or service marks are listed below. In addition, terms suspected of being trademarks or service marks have been appropriately capitalized. Waite Group Press cannot attest to the accuracy of this information. Use of a term in this book should not be regarded as affecting the validity of any trademark or service mark.

Macintosh and Quadra are trademarks of Apple Computer Inc.

Convolvotron is the trademark of Crystal River Engineering

MicroCosm is the trademark of VPL Research, Inc.

Virtuality is the trademark of CyberStudio

Amiga is the trademark of Commodore Business Machines

Hand Master is the trademark of Exos

Power Glove is a trademark of Mattell Toys

DataGlove is a trademark of VPL Research, Inc.

CrystalEyes is a trademark of StereoGraphics Corp.

MiG-29 is the copyright of DoMark

Superscape is the copyright of Dimension International

Virtual Reality Studio is the copyright of DoMark

Stare-EO is the trademark of Micro Synectic

Waite Group Press is a registered trademark of The Waite Group, Inc.

Figures 2.6, 2.7, 2.8, 2.9 and 2.10 reprinted from *Stereoscopic Cinema* and *CrystalEyes* by permission of the author, Lenny Lipton.

Contents

Foreword

Before turning my attention to the world of virtual experience, I spent fourteen years programming and managing the development of games for personal computers, video game consoles, and arcade machines. When making hiring decisions, I generally looked for specific experience on the target platform. For example, if the target platform was video game consoles, such as Sega or Nintendo, I would look for cartridge programmers. For disk-based games to run on IBM PCs or Macintoshes, I would look for disk programmers with experience on the specific hardware.

When I started developing software for virtual reality systems, I realized how similar those traditional platforms really are. They all use two-dimensional flat screen displays to represent visual images. They all use built-in speakers to generate the audio. And they all use combinations of joysticks, mice, or keyboards as input devices. There is no significant difference between floppy disks, hard disks, CD ROM optical disks, cartridges, or ROM chips. These are simply storage devices.

Virtual reality systems, on the other hand, use true 3-D sound and audio. The visual display is no longer a flat two-dimensional screen, but a true stereoscopic 3-D display. Input devices are no longer simple joysticks or mice. Now your head, arms, and body are the input devices. The programmer has to read the X, Y, and Z positions of your head and its elevation, roll, and azimuth. He or she has to use the changes in multiple readings to compute vectored motion and velocity for all these parts of your body.

Virtual reality has resulted in a dramatic retooling of game development systems. At Spectrum HoloByte we are spending almost as much time creating new tools to help us develop virtual reality software as we spend developing the software itself.

Virtual Reality Playhouse is an excellent introduction to the technology that is used in virtual reality systems. Together with its disk of sample programs, it should provide a solid foundation for anyone wishing to learn more about this fascinating field.

A. J. Redmer
Executive Director, Virtuality Group
Spectrum HoloByte & CyberStudio Inc.

Preface

The problem with virtual reality is its dependence on complicated (and expensive) hardware. A "desktop" virtual reality system (essentially a high-end PC with special hardware and software) can cost $10,000 to $15,000 or more. A full-fledged virtual reality system with a head-mounted display and glove input devices can cost upwards of $50,000, not counting the specialized software and the personnel needed to make it work. And if you are interested in virtual reality for entertainment, your only choice is to spend $65,000 to buy a Virtuality arcade game, or else spend a dollar per minute playing it in an arcade. None of this is much help for people who just want to browse and experiment with this new technology.

Hence *Virtual Reality Playhouse.* While this little book does not pretend to be a substitute for professional virtual reality systems, neither does it require a major investment on the part of those merely interested in doing a little high-tech tinkering. The disk of demonstration software included with the book lets you explore an industrial park from a first-person point of view, observe objects through 3-D glasses and rotate them on the screen, fly a MiG fighter, or play games that are set in a 3-D environment. And if you are technically inclined, you can learn how to modify an inexpensive glove input device to work with your PC, or a pair of LCD shutter glasses to work with your PC or Macintosh computer.

Dear Reader:

No development in recent memory, save maybe the PC itself, has as much potential appeal as Virtual Reality. Why is this? Perhaps it's because VR promises to turn our PCs into customizable worlds that let us bend the very laws of nature. For example, with a PC-based virtual reality display your cursor moves not just left and right, or up and down, but in and out of the screen. With a simple data glove and you can reach into your screen, grab objects, and move them around. Since the viewpoint of your world is under software control you can now walk through a building, see how light comes through the windows or watch the ways a view changes. VR may be the first real paradigm shift since the hologram, for in a way it finally gives a practical use for stereo vision on the PC.

For the past year we have been investigating the technology of virtual reality and considering how it will affect the world of computers. We've donned helmet mounted displays, pulled on our data gloves, and dived into incredible worlds of imagination. Think about flying in a world by pointing your index finger in the air, or grabbing objects that have mass but no weight! When we came back to "real" reality we knew VR was the dawn of a new age. Don't get us wrong. Some of what we saw was crude; sort of like a 3-D maneuverable game of Pong. But you will recall how the crude block-like Pong has evolved into incredibly sophisticated and powerful CAD programs that go far beyond our first videogame experiences. Virtual Reality on the PC is at a similar junction.

WAITE GROUP
PRESS™

As a publisher with a mission to bring you the latest technology in a simple and friendly manner, the big problem was how to encapsulate the new frontier of virtual reality in a book and disk and give a real feeling for what is possible. We know that there is not yet a large installed base of Helmet Mounted Displays and Data Gloves. So what we've done is to find a collection of graphics programs that gives you a sampling of this bold new world. The programs on the disk present some recent VR demos, 3-D simulations, games, details on building LCD shuttering glasses, etc. Essentially this book is a weekend of fun. For those who are interested in this subject we are following up this book with some astounding virtual reality titles and software. And we will continue to stake ourselves out at the cutting edge of technology to bring you books on subjects you can only imagine! Fill out and return our Reader Satisfaction Card at the back of this book to obtain a catalog and see what's in store!

Sincerely,

Mitchell Waite

Mitchell Waite
Publisher

200 Tamal Plaza   Corte Madera   California   94925   415-924-2575   Fax 415-924-2576

About this Book

Virtual Reality Playhouse examines the foundations of virtual reality, and provides some practical, hands-on experience with software similar to that used by virtual reality systems. Part One surveys the underlying technology, showing how the senses can be tricked into believing they are experiencing an alternate reality. Here we examine the technology behind head-mounted displays, glove input devices, and the million-dollar flying and driving simulators.

Part Two describes the software included with the book, showing you how to install it and how to use it to experience some of the virtual reality phenomena. Try to find your way back to Earth from an alien world, explore an industrial park, or fly a MiG fighter. Look through 3-D glasses at wireframe objects that appear to float in front of your computer display, or experience the 3-D effect without glasses. We think you'll have fun playing with the software, and taking a peek at alternate realities. Welcome to cyberspace!

PART 1
WHAT IS
VIRTUAL
REALITY?

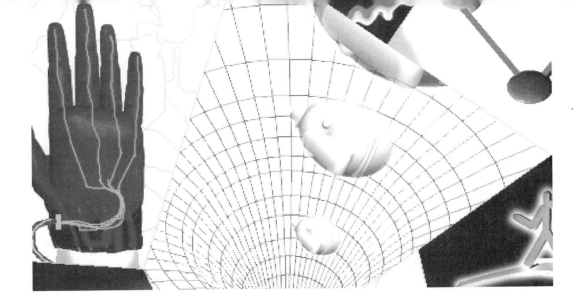

You step onto the platform and lower the large, donut-shaped ring around your body. You strap the belt around your middle, and put on the head-mounted display. In a few moments, you start to experience a world that you know isn't real, yet responds to your movements as though it were.

Move your head to the right, and the scene changes, bringing into view parts of the terrain that were previously hidden. Press the top button on the joystick you are holding, and you glide effortlessly forward.

Suddenly you see the other player emerge from behind a pillar. You quickly take aim and press the trigger on the joystick, knowing that in this ruthless virtual world, it's kill or be killed. You score a direct hit, and your opponent disintegrates into a dozen pieces. No time to gloat, however, because the heartbeat you hear is that of the pterodactyl swooping down from above, close and menacing.

Too late! The creature grabs you in its huge claws and drags you off to its lair. You too explode into a dozen pieces. Chalk up one more round for the pterodactyl.

You are playing Dactyl Nightmare, the virtual reality game created by W. Industries to run on their Virtuality machines. Although you are standing on a platform three feet in diameter, the visual and auditory feedback you receive from the head-mounted display is telling you otherwise. What you see (and hear) is a world made up of floating platforms connected by narrow staircases, and strange doorways that lead to nowhere.

And even though your opponent is standing on a similar platform a short distance away, you are both sharing the same virtual space, stalking each other while avoiding the ever-present threat of the pterodactyl hovering overhead. You each experience the virtual world from your own peculiar point of view, interacting with it and with each other as if it were real.

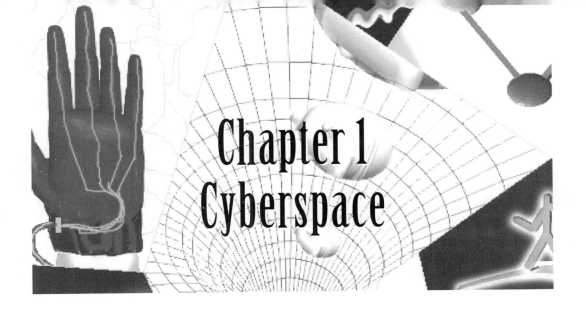

Chapter 1
Cyberspace

Alternate reality is nothing new. One could argue that Daniel Defoe's *Robinson Crusoe,* which is often credited as the first novel published in the English language, is an early example of alternate reality, since the reader experiences another world through the eyes of the main character. Although what you are actually seeing when you read a book is a collection of complex symbols, your imagination helps you experience the feelings and images that keep you turning the pages.

Movies are another kind of alternate reality. They draw our emotions into the plot and dynamics, so that we often forget that what we are actually seeing is nothing more than a dark screen illuminated by occasional flashes of light. Imagination takes a back seat to neurophysiology in the darkened theater, since the images and emotions of the alternate reality are fed to you directly. All your brain needs to do at the movie theater is fuse the series of static images into continuous movement, while you sit back and enjoy the show.

Unlike pulp- and celluloid-based media, which depend on plots and characters to draw you into their alternate realities, virtual reality envelops you in an artificial world that "feels" real, that responds to your every move much as the real world does. You feel as if you have become a character in a movie, and the plot follows your actions. Imagination again takes a back seat to neurophysiology in a virtual reality system, where the emphasis is on the direct stimulation of the senses to create the experience of another world.

Virtual reality, or "cyberspace" as it is often called (after the term in William Gibson's novel *Neuromancer*), takes alternate reality a step further by introducing a computer as a mediator, or imagination enhancer. A typical virtual reality system consists of one or more input devices (such as a joystick, a steering wheel, or a body harness), several forms of output (such as light, sound, and pressure), and a computer to manage all the data. For example, you might be sitting in the cockpit of a race car with your hands on the steering wheel and your foot on the gas pedal, staring straight ahead at a computer display made to look like a car windshield. The computer monitors your input (the pressure on the gas pedal, the degree of turn of the steering wheel) and adjusts the image on the display accordingly.

Thus, as you turn the wheel to the left, the computer displays a series of images commensurate with a left turn in a race car. (Some more sophisticated systems would also tilt the cockpit to the right, using the pressure on the right side of your body to simulate the g-forces operating during a left turn.) Likewise, as you press harder on the gas pedal, the computer uses that input to speed up the rate at which it displays the images, giving you the impression that you are moving faster. Figure 1.1 shows the relationship between input, output, and the CPU on a driving simulator.

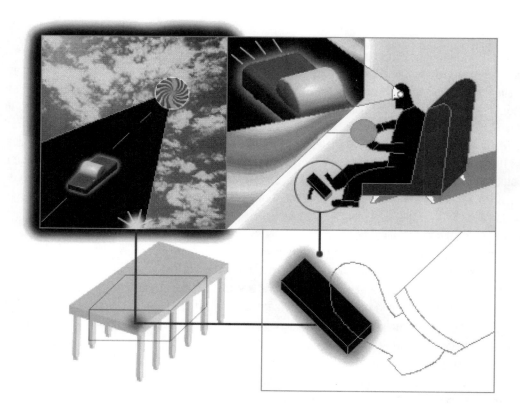

Figure 1.1 *When you depress the gas pedal in this driving simulator,*
the display speeds up the frame rate to give the impression that you are moving faster

THE ELEMENTS OF VIRTUAL REALITY

Although there are no hard and fast rules about what a virtual reality system should and shouldn't have, the best systems make use of three basic elements: immersion, navigation, and manipulation.

IMMERSION

To be immersed in a virtual reality system is to feel that you are experiencing an alternate reality from the inside, not merely observing it through a window. It is as though you are *inside* a video game, dealing with the other characters, who are now life-size and who can appear behind you, to your left or right, or even flying over your head. (Recall the movie *Tron,* where the main character finds himself inside the computer game that he programmed, battling the other characters in the game.)

Immersion is primarily a function of hardware. Some virtual reality systems, such as the Virtuality machine that runs Dactyl Nightmare, use a head-mounted display (or HMD) instead of a standard computer display to stimulate the visual sense. By presenting a slightly different image to each of your eyes, the head-mounted display uses the phenomenon of *binocular parallax* to create 3-D effects, adding further realism to the virtual world. (We'll be covering the physiological basis of virtual reality systems a little later in the book.) The HMD also stimulates your auditory sense through its stereo headphones, giving you cues about the source and direction of the sound by presenting the sound to one ear a split second before the other.

The head-mounted display can also monitor your head movements, feeding a stream of data to the computer about your head's position and orientation in three-dimensional space, or "three-space." The computer in turn adjusts the display on the HMD, resulting in visual stimulation that is synchronized with your head movements.

Some virtual reality systems use additional input devices, such as gloves that can sense your hand's position and orientation. Known as *glove input devices,* or *data gloves,* these act like the head-mounted displays, providing additional data to the computer. Figure 1.2 diagrams a typical virtual reality system.

In an immersion environment, you sit inside a cockpit and fly or drive using a steering wheel and foot pedals. You view the virtual world through the head-mounted display, while the cockpit sways and banks as you maneuver around the imaginary course. You feel as though you are actually flying or driving. The virtual reality machine has taken control of your senses, and has cut you off from "true" reality.

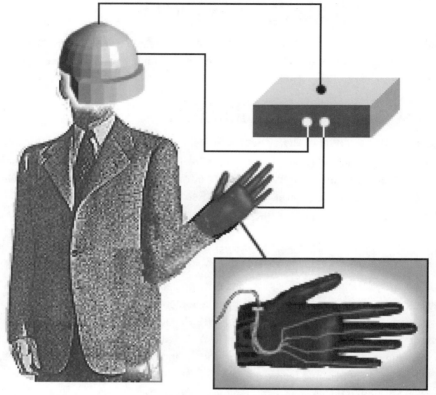

Figure 1.2 Typical virtual reality system, with head-mounted display and data gloves

Sensorama

Morton Heilig's Sensorama machine, a multisensory device designed in 1962 to stimulate the user's sense of touch, vision, hearing, and smell, is an example of a non-computer-based virtual reality system using immersion techniques. The user sat on a stool facing a small rear-projection movie screen and held on to a pair of handlebars (see Figure 1.3).

Sensorama took the user on a ride through several scenes, including a bike ride through Brooklyn and over sand dunes in California. It stimulated the tactile senses through vibrating handlebars and a seat that lurched as the "bike" took off. It stimulated the audio and visual senses by presenting the user with film clips and synchronized sounds, and the olfactory sense by blowing aromas through small jets aimed at the user's face. The ride ended with a visit to a belly-dance show complete with the smell of cheap perfume.

Although the Sensorama experience was based on old technology, it did succeed in immersing the user in a virtual world for a brief time. Heilig's machine was never produced in any quantity, and only the prototype remains in existence today. Today, the first non-computer-based virtual reality system sits in a shed somewhere in Los Angeles.

Star Tours

The Disneyland attraction Star Tours provides a present-day example of a step towards immersion. The audience in the Star Tours ride experiences a white-knuckle journey into space as the bumbling robot pilot narrowly avoids collisions and disasters. Although the sensations of rapid acceleration and deceleration are startlingly realistic, the Star Tours pod never actually goes anywhere in the real-world sense, for the entire trip takes place on the ground. The sensations of motion and gravity are created by the rapid pitching and tilting of the seats and of the pod itself, while multiple-channel stereophonic sound adds a further layer of realism.

Immersion is the difference between viewing an alternate reality through a window (whether the alternate reality is in the form of a book, a movie, or a traditional video game) and viewing it from the inside, as a participant. Immersion is the single most important element of a virtual reality system, and is what makes the reality "virtual."

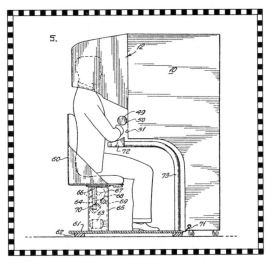

Figure 1.3 Morton Heilig's Sensorama took the user on a "ride" through a variety of locales

Navigation

Immersion tricks you into thinking you are in an alternate reality, while navigation gives you the opportunity to explore it. Navigation is the ability to move about in a computer-generated cyberspace, exploring and interacting with it apparently at will. Naturally, this doesn't mean you actually go anywhere; it's the feeling that you can move about that makes a world "virtual." A virtual world is like a dream: You can be lying in bed in the real world, yet be exploring dungeons and magical kingdoms, flying intercontinental passenger jets, or running down the street in your shorts in the virtual world.

Although Heilig's Sensorama did succeed in immersing the user in its virtual world, the experience was nonetheless passive, since the user was only a passenger on the ride. This is not to downplay the machine (or its inventor) in any way. The technology for a navigable virtual reality system was simply not available in 1962, and wouldn't be for at least another twenty-five years. To include navigation control in Sensorama using the technology of 1962 would have required a different film strip for every crossroad on the ride, and some means of switching quickly from one strip to the next, a task that would be challenging even today.

In fact, the same criticism could be leveled at the Star Tours ride, since it too provides immersion without navigation. That the criticism is not valid is evidenced by the intensity of the Star Tours ride. Navigation in that case would be a very thin layer of icing on an already substantial cake.

The industrial flying and driving simulators (with price tags well into the millions of dollars) often provide both the substantial cake and that layer of icing, since they successfully create a virtual world that can be as realistic as the real one. Mercedes Benz's truck driving simulator, for example, is so realistic that an operator told to drive the truck off the road is often unable to do so—not merely unwilling, but actually unable. Now *that's* virtual reality.

While we weren't able to shoehorn one of those truck driving simulators into the pocket in the back of this book, we were able to squeeze in one or two programs that let you navigate around virtual worlds. Superscape lets you explore an industrial park using a mouse and keyboard, while Lemme Out of Here! challenges you to find a way off a mysterious planet and back to Earth. You can find these and other virtual reality-related programs on the disk in the back of the book.

Manipulation

The third variable that gives a virtual reality system its realistic edge is the user's ability to manipulate the environment in some fashion. Manipulation is simply the ability to reach out and knock on a virtual door, or shoot at a virtual foe, and have the virtual world respond appropriately. For example, you might put on a data glove and reach out and rotate an object in your virtual field of vision. The object would respond as though it were a real object being rotated in the real world.

Ideally, you would "feel" the virtual object as you rotated it, by means of little tactile stimulators (known as *tactors*) embedded in the glove. We'll discuss tactile feedback a bit more under Touch and Proprioception, Chapter 2.

In the two-player version of Dactyl Nightmare, you and your opponent are stalking each other in the virtual world, while avoiding the ever-present menace of the pterodactyl. A successful hit (whether of the opponent or the pterodactyl) results in a spectacular explosion. You know you've just had an effect on your virtual environment.

In the game Lemme Out of Here!, you can manipulate various objects in your environment by clicking on them with the right mouse button. Click on a doorknob, for example, and the door opens. Click on a piece of rope, and you pick it up and retain it as part of your inventory. The program Wire 3-D also lets you manipulate objects on the screen, and you can do so in 3-D, using the 3-D glasses we've included with the book. Press the directional arrows on your keyboard, and watch the three-dimensional object rotate, looking as though it is floating somewhere inside your monitor.

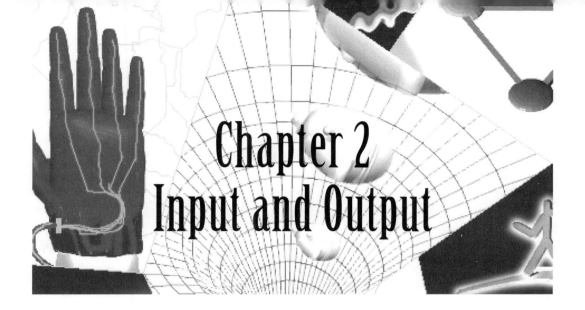

Chapter 2
Input and Output

An effective virtual reality system requires a close correspondence between *input* (the data that is fed into the computer) and *output* (the data that comes out). In most cases, the kind of data that feeds a virtual reality system consists of signals generated by an input device of some sort, such as a glove, a head-mounted display, or a steering wheel and foot pedals.

We can distinguish between this kind of input device, which has some relationship with the virtual world being explored, and other input devices, such as keyboards or mice, which do not. For example, if the virtual world is one that the user manipulates by hand, picking up objects and moving them around, then a data glove is the most appropriate input device. In that case, a keyboard would be less appropriate, since it would not help maintain the illusion of the virtual world. Similarly, if the virtual world is one that the user explores by walking around, then a pressure-sensitive floor would be most appropriate.

Because the input side of the formula is hardware-dependent, requiring sensitive (and expensive) monitoring equipment, the software we've included with *Virtual Reality Playhouse* emphasizes the output side. So while you won't get to use a head-mounted display to navigate around an office complex, you will be able to move around using the keyboard or joystick.

INPUT DEVICES

The following are some examples of input devices used by typical virtual reality systems. You don't have to have all of them, but the more you have, the more realistic the effect.

GLOVE INPUT DEVICES

A glove input device is a glove that uses electronics to sense the position and orientation of the hand wearing it. As your hand moves around in three-space, the glove sends a stream of electronic data to the computer in the form of three-dimensional coordinates. The computer then uses the data to manipulate an object on the display. For example, you might move your hand as though you were rotating a cube in space. The computer uses the data generated by the glove to rotate a cube on the screen, perfectly synchronized with your hand movements (see Figure 2.1). The effect can be quite realistic, especially if you are wearing 3-D glasses and the output display uses double-image 3-D techniques (more about this later).

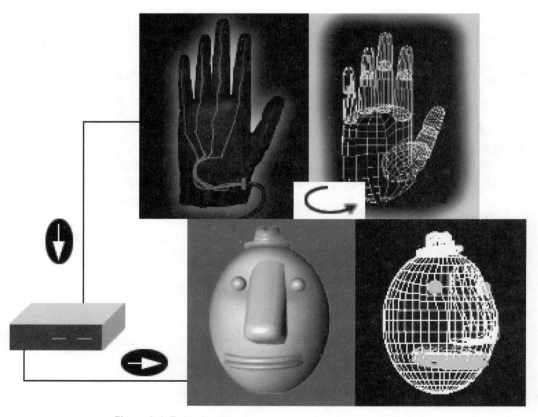

Figure 2.1 *Twist the data glove, and the display responds in kind*

Figure 2.2 Optical fibers determine the flexing and bending of fingers

Although various technologies have been used with gloves to sense flexing and movement, the most elegant (for instance, the VPL DataGlove) makes use of fiber optics. With this technique, the glove incorporates a network of optical fibers (the kind used in modern telephone lines) stretched along the fingers. The technique involves shining a light of a known intensity into one end of the network of fibers, and then measuring its intensity as it comes out the other. Some of the fibers are etched at the finger and knuckle joints, which results in a loss of light when the fingers are bent. The light emerging from the end of the etched fibers is compared against the light emerging from the unetched fibers (the "control group," if you like) (see Figure 2.2). The computer uses this data to determine which joints were flexed and to what extent, and then adjusts the display accordingly. This is how the VPL DataGlove works.

Another technique, used by Exos's Dexterous Hand Master, involves an intricate exoskeleton of magnets and sensors that measure the bending angle of each joint in the hand. Several sets of magnets and sensors are connected to each finger with Velcro bands, making the whole thing look like some extraterrestrial robotic device (see Figure 2.3). You don't just slip one of these on, you install it with great care and attention—which is what you would expect of a precision instrument costing around $15,000.

The choice between the VPL DataGlove and the Exos Hand Master is a matter of task. The Data-Glove emphasizes comfort and style (no protruding sensors to snag on your mohair sweater) at a

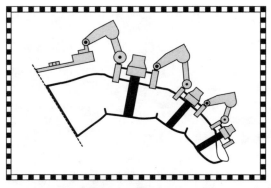

Figure 2.3 *Exos's exoskeletal glove measures finger flexing by means of magnets and sensors*

relatively low price of $8,800. The Hand Master, on the other hand (oops, sorry), emphasizes exacting precision with some small trade-off in convenience.

For the Super Mario set, who require convenience, durability, and economy in their data gloves, Mattell used the Power Glove for the Nintendo Entertainment System. The Power Glove takes an entirely different approach to measure hand position and orientation, using strain gauges at the finger and knuckle joints to monitor flexing. The strain gauges are constructed of polyester strips coated with a special ink that changes resistance when it is flexed. Five strips monitor flexing of the five fingers.

Even though the Power Glove does not provide the precision of either the DataGlove or the Hand Master, it can still track your hand movements to within a quarter of an inch, even at a distance of five feet from the display. And at under $100, you can arm (oops, sorry again) an entire convention of gamers for the price of one Hand Master.

Absolute Location

The use of strain gauges or optical fibers can only monitor the hand's position and orientation, not its absolute location in three-space. For absolute location, some additional technique is required. The Power Glove emits an ultrasonic signal that is picked up by a receiver on the display—actually, three receivers, making use of triangulation to pinpoint the glove's location (see Figure 2.4).

In addition to absolute location, the receivers can also monitor the degree of roll and pitch of the glove.

VPL and Exos both use Polhemus's tracker technology for their high-end gloves. This involves the use of magnetic fields and sensors that can detect the glove's location within the magnetic field. This is also the approach taken by Ascension, another developer of position detection technology.

HEAD-MOUNTED DISPLAYS

The most effective (and dramatic) virtual reality input device is the head-mounted display. This device, which handles both the input and output sides of the virtual reality formula, fits over the user's head, like a helmet, or is suspended from the ceiling. The HMD monitors the side-to-side and up-

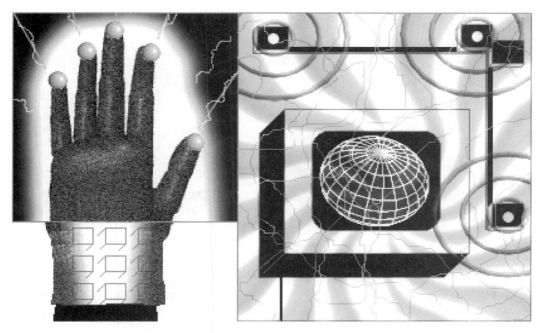

Figure 2.4 *Mattell's Power Glove uses a triangulation technique to pinpoint the glove's absolute location in three-space*

and-down head movements, and sends a corresponding stream of data to the computer about its position. The computer uses this data to generate stereo images of the virtual world.

The stereo images are then sent to the pair of miniaturized displays (the output side of the virtual reality formula) that are an integral part of the HMD. Because each eye gets its own image, and because the images differ slightly from one another, the effect is one of viewing a three-dimensional world. (Figure 2.5 shows a head-mounted display made by Virtual Research of Sunnyvale, California.) And because the stereo images are synchronized with head movements, the effect can be quite realistic (or, more commonly, "way cool"), giving the impression of actually moving about in an alternate reality. We'll look at the stereoscopic aspect of this technique a little later (see 3-D Effects, below), when we discuss stereoscopic vision and 3-D glasses.

Absolute Location

Most HMDs monitor not only the head's orientation, but its absolute location as well. With the addition of this kind of data, the virtual world becomes very real.

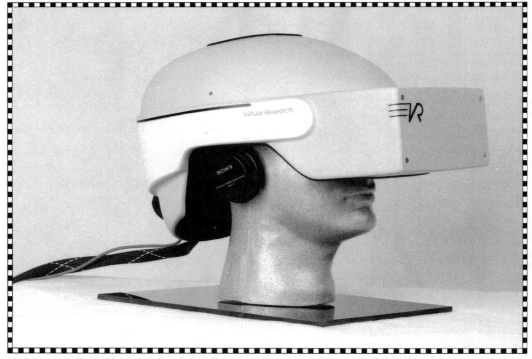

Figure 2.5 *This head-mounted display from Virtual Research includes twin displays and built-in stereo headphones*

One way to monitor absolute location is through the use of a transmitter mounted on the HMD and a receiver mounted on or near the computer. As you move around, the computer receives a stream of data, which it uses to modify the size of the objects in your field of view. The addition of absolute data can help create an artificial reality that appears as deep and dynamic as the real world.

Another approach makes use of magnetic sensors and a magnetic field surrounding the HMD. As you move around within the magnetic field, the sensors track your position and report it to the computer.

HMDs are still too expensive to become the joystick of the 1990s (otherwise we would have included an inflatable one with this book). VPL Research, one of the pioneers of the data glove, recently announced a complete virtual reality system called MicroCosm. MicroCosm is based on a Macintosh Quadra 900™ and consists of an HMD, one or two DataGloves, and a "black box" that controls all the input and output. At $58,000, VPL's MicroCosm is a bargain compared to other virtual reality systems, but it's still a little too pricey for a stocking stuffer.

OUTPUT

The most important form of output from a virtual reality system is visible light, either from a standard monitor (as in the race car driving simulator described earlier) or from the binocular displays of an HMD. Clearly, the greater the variety in output, the more realistic the effect; most virtual reality systems also use sound and skin pressure in addition to light to propagate the illusion of an alternate world.

LIGHT

Our eyes provide us with information about the quality and quantity of light in our immediate environment. Working together, a pair of eyes can provide more information about the size and relative location of objects in our field of view than two eyes working independently.

Anyone who has labored through Psychology 101 knows about the visual cues the brain uses to determine the size and location of objects in three-space. For example, given a light source behind the observer, the brain interprets a dimly lit object as farther away than a brighter one. Likewise, an object that appears smaller will be judged to be farther away than one appearing bigger, as will one that appears behind another. These *monocular* cues, which don't depend on a pair of eyes working in tandem, are relatively simple to program into a virtual reality system (see Figure 2.6).

More interesting for virtual reality are the visual cues that depend on the working of both eyes together. These *binocular* cues are the basis for stereoscopic vision, which in turn is one of the fundamental elements of a virtual reality system that uses an HMD.

3-D EFFECTS

Two significant things happen when eyes focus on an object. First, the eyes converge so that the object is in the direct line of sight of each eye as shown in Figure 2.7). This *binocular convergence* occurs through the action of the muscles controlling eye movement, and provides feedback to the brain about the relative distance of the object—the greater the convergence, the closer the object. The brain relies on the *proprioceptive* feedback from these muscles to make its determination of relative distance: the greater the tension in these muscles, the greater the convergence, and so on. (Proprioception is simply the brain's perception of the body's state, such as its posture or orientation.)

Second, each eye receives a slightly different image of the object—the left eye sees a little more of the left side of the object than does the right eye, which sees more of the right side. The brain uses

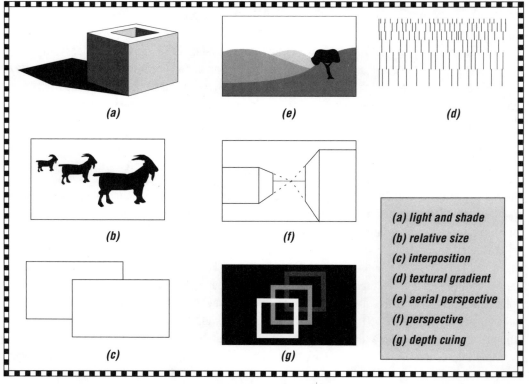

Figure 2.6 *Monocular depth cues.*

this *binocular parallax* to make a further interpretation of the relative distance of the object — the greater the disparity between the two images, the closer the object. Both of these factors form the basis for *stereopsis,* the binocular sense of depth.

Let's see how early experiments with 3-D vision have contributed to the evolution of the HMD of today.

From Stereoscopes to HMDs

The history of the technology leading up to the HMD can be traced directly to Sir Charles Wheatstone and his mirror stereoscope of 1833. Wheatstone's device resembled a pair of binoculars with wings. The "wings" were actually mirrors reflecting each of the two images to the appropriate eye. Unlike the later stereoscopes, which used a single card with the two images side by side, Wheatstone's images were on separate cards, and were placed at the sides of the viewer rather than in front (see Figure 2.8).

Wheatstone's device, and that of the later stereoscopes, was fine for individual viewing, but was not workable for audiences greater than one. A different approach was needed to make the 3-D effect available to larger groups of people.

Figure 2.7 *The eyes converge to focus on an image; the closer the image, the greater the binocular convergence*

Anaglyphs

The so-called anaglyphic technique was first demonstrated in 1858 by a man by the name of D'Almeida, who used red and green filters over the lenses of both the projectors and the glasses. The idea behind his demonstration was simple. First project the right-hand image through a green filter, and the left-hand image through a red one. Now put a green filter over the left eye, to render the right-hand image invisible to that eye, and a red filter over the right eye. Because the green lens cancels out the green image, and the red lens cancels out the red image, the result is that each eye gets its own unique image, and the brain fuses the two to create the effect of depth.

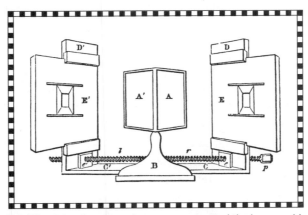

Figure 2.8 *Wheatstone's mirror stereoscope mounted the images side by side*

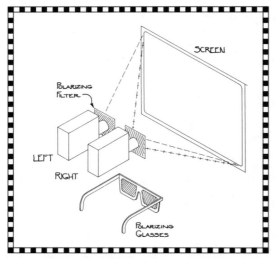

Figure 2.9 *Light polarized in one direction is rendered invisible by filter polarized in the opposite direction*

3-D Movies

The red-and-green filter approach was the one adopted by Hollywood in 1937 for its first 3-D movie, aptly named *Third-Dimension Murder.* Although moderately successful, its limitations soon became apparent as Hollywood started moving into the world of color. (Since this technology used red and green filters to separate the two images, it would not work with color films.) The breakthrough came in 1952 with the release of *Bwana Devil,* the industry's first color 3-D movie.

Bwana Devil and the 3-D movies that followed it used polarizing filters on the projectors and on the lenses worn by the audience. The idea behind it was identical to D'Almeida's red and green filters, except that polarized light was used to separate the left and right images. The left image was polarized in one direction (say, vertically), while the right image was polarized in the other (horizontally). The left lens was transparent for vertically polarized light, but opaque for horizontally polarized light, with the opposite being true for the right lens. Figure 2.9 shows a typical 3-D projection technique using polarizing filters.

Computers Can Do It Too

The popularity of 3-D movies waned almost as quickly as it waxed. Since 1954 only a handful of movies have been produced using 3-D techniques, compared to the hundreds produced in the two years before that. But Hollywood's loss would prove to be Silicon Valley's gain, as software developers took up the cause in the 1980s. So far, a handful of commercial products have been launched that make use of 3-D technology (such as The Waite Group's Fractal Creations, which comes with 3-D glasses and software that generates stereoscopic images). Most 3-D software uses red-and-blue filtered glasses to create the 3-D effect, thereby restricting the output to monochromatic images.

Sega's LCD Shuttering System

The 3-D glasses available for Sega's Master Game System use an entirely different technique to project a unique image to each eye. Instead of having both the left and right images present at the same time and using filters to selectively project the appropriate image to each eye, Sega's technique involves switching the screen image between the left and right views sixty times every second, synchronized with LCD "shutters" in the glasses. When the left eye image is visible on the screen (for one-sixtieth of a second), the right lens is opaque; and when the right eye image is visible, the left lens is opaque. The brain fuses the left and right images into a stereo view.

If you own a pair of these shuttering LCD glasses, you can build a little circuit board, or modify the existing Sega board, allowing you to use these glasses on a Macintosh or an IBM-compatible computer. You can find instructions for creating or modifying the circuit boards for an IBM PC-compatible in Chapter 12.

StereoGraphics's Pi-Cell Technology

While Sega's glasses aim at the budget-conscious, those available from StereoGraphics Corporation in San Rafael, California represent the high end. StereoGraphics's glasses feature state-of-the-art pi-

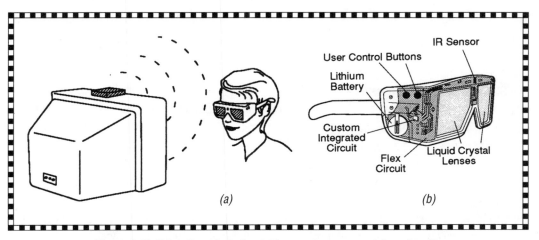

Figure 2.10 *StereoGraphics's CrystalEyes system uses an infrared emitter on the monitor (a) and LCD lenses (b) to create the 3D effect on a monitor*

cell LCD technology, with infrared transmitting and receiving capability. The infrared transmitter sits atop the monitor, and sends the signals that turn the LCD shutters on and off, eliminating the need for cables between glasses and monitor. Figure 2.10 shows StereoGraphics's CrystalEyes system.

The result is full-color flicker-free stereoscopic vision, whether it is used with a closed-circuit television system or with computer-generated images. The effect is extremely lifelike—that is, until you move your head and change your perspective.

Head Movement Is a Fact of Real Life

The problem with most 3-D technology is the inappropriate and unrealistic feedback you get when you move your head while viewing a 3-D image. Try the following experiment for yourself, and you'll see what we mean:

Look out of a window (or down a long hallway), and move your head to the left or the right. You notice that objects closer to you are displaced a greater distance than objects farther away, while the most distant objects are displaced hardly at all. This phenomenon is known as *movement parallax,* and was first used by Walt Disney in his classic *Snow White and the Seven Dwarfs* to create a sense of depth in the scrolling backgrounds. (Prior to *Snow White,* animated backgrounds were a simple flat backdrop that scrolled uniformly, irrespective of apparent distance from the observer.)

The problem with 3-D images (computer-generated or otherwise) is an absence of movement parallax; moving your head side to side while viewing a 3-D image does not result in any relative displacement of the objects in the picture. And it does not provide any new information about the scene either, such as data about the sides or the top and bottom of an object. Instead, the whole image shifts in a strange way.

StereoGraphics incorporates a tiny Logitech 3-D ultrasonic mouse transmitter in a pair of the StereoGraphics LCD glasses. A corresponding receiver, using triangulation techniques, receives the sound pulses and calculates the transmitter's location in three-space (see Figure 2.11). Used with StereoGraphics's LCD glasses, Logitech's 3-D mouse system keeps track of the absolute location of the glasses, and adjusts the screen image to fit. Moving your head to the right reveals more of the right side of the object, while moving your head up reveals more of the top of the object.

One of the software demos we've included with this book, Wire 3-D, lets you rotate a 3-D object on the screen as you view it through 3-D glasses. Try moving your head from side to side as you view the various objects, and see how the feedback doesn't quite match the real-life experience. Now imagine moving your head to the right and seeing more of the right side of the object, and you'll get the idea about StereoGraphics's system.

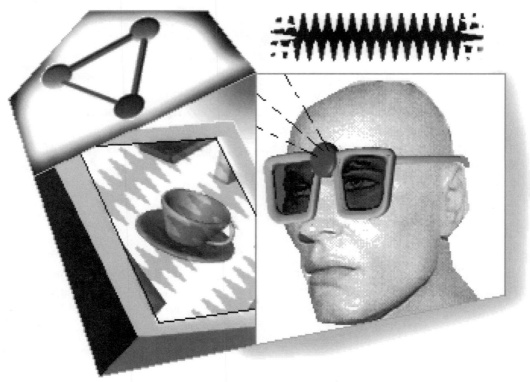

Figure 2.11 *The triangular receiver localizes the glasses in three-space to create real-world feedback on the display*

3-D SOUND

As the audio industry discovered in the 1950s, the visual world was not the only one that existed in three dimensions. People have two ears for a reason: [Two ears allow the brain to localize sound in three-space, by taking account of the fact that a sound usually reaches one ear a split second before it reaches the other.] These tiny time lags were the basis for the "new" stereophonic sound of the 1950s, which was recorded using two microphones to mimic the two ears of the listener. Of course, the brain has an additional sense of aural depth perception, so you can distinguish sounds above your head from below, for instance.

While the audio industry continues to pursue its goal of faithful reproduction of music (hence "high fidelity"), the computer industry is pursuing a different one: creating or enhancing a virtual world through auditory stimulation. Imagine walking around in a virtual world, listening to your footsteps as they echo down a long corridor. Somewhere to your right a voice whispers, "Pssst!" You stop and turn to look at a bent figure hiding in the doorway. She (for it is an old woman dressed in rags) unfolds a crumpled piece of paper and hands it to you.

The inclusion of sound to a virtual reality system adds an extra dimension of reality to the environment, just as the addition of synchronized speech breathed new life to the movies of the 1930s. A device developed by Crystal River Engineering and dubbed the Convolvotron uses 128 or more processors to re-create a three-dimensional aural environment. Commercially, the use of 3-D audio is usually confined to two or four channels, as in the Virtuality machines now installed in video arcades.

TOUCH AND PROPRIOCEPTION

The sense of touch lets you interact with and gather information about the environment by feeling it with your fingers or other parts of your body. Imagine your virtual hand reaching out into cyberspace and clutching an object suspended there, or reaching out and pressing a doorbell, and actually feeling the object with your fingertips. You would *see* your virtual hand pressing the doorbell on the display, and you would *feel* the tactile pressure on your index finger as you did so.

Tactile Feedback

The technology is now available to make this a reality. One approach makes use of shape memory metals, alloys that "remember" their original shape and regain it when heated. These metals are the basis for the tactile stimulators, or *tactors*, that are embedded in the glove worn by the user. When the computer detects a collision between your virtual hand and the virtual object on the display, it sends an electrical current to the tactor, causing the metal strip to change shape moving a peri which applies pressure to your fingertip. Figure 2.12 shows the tactile feedback device available from Xtensory.

With the inclusion of tactors, a glove input device can also double as an output device, giving you tactile feedback on your relationship to the virtual world. Imagine reaching out and feeling the side of a virtual cube suspended in cyberspace, and feeling the tactile sensation end as you reach the edge of the cube. Or, imagine running your fingers across a rough virtual texture, causing the tactors to turn rapidly on and off to re-create the sensation of the same action in the real world.

Figure 2.12 Xtensory's tactile feedback gloves let you feel the virtual object you are seeing on the display

Force Feedback

It's one thing to reach out and press a virtual doorbell and feel pressure on your fingertip. It's quite another to reach out and grasp a virtual object that is supposed to be solid. In that case, tactile pressure on your fingertips would not be enough to reproduce the sensation of grasping a solid object. What you need is force feedback, letting you know if the virtual object is hard, soft, or malleable.

Force feedback gloves are a little more touchy than those providing simple tactile feedback. For one thing, they must rely on some kind of exoskeleton to provide the necessary resistance to mimic solidity. As your fingers grasp the virtual object, the exoskeleton would stiffen, becoming completely rigid in the case of a hard object, or springy in the case of a malleable one. The problem is that the exoskeleton would feel cumbersome most of the time, and its inherent bulkiness would get in the way. We await the advance of technology on this one.

Proprioception

Another aspect of the sense of touch (and the likeliest candidate for what may be a "sixth sense") is *proprioception,* the feedback our body gives us about its current state, posture, or position.

For example, when you bend over to pick something up off the floor, your body lets you know that you are bent over, not only through visual cues but also through the sensory feedback associated with that posture. You feel the effects of gravity in your inner ear, the straining of your muscles, blood flowing to your head, and so on. Clearly, there is a certain feeling associated with bending over that is different from the feeling associated with walking forward or sitting down.

This proprioceptive sense is as important in virtual reality systems as the tactile sense, since a critical part of the illusion is the user's perception of his or her relation to the virtual world. To a blind-folded user, or to one wearing an HMD, there is little difference between walking on a treadmill and walking on a sidewalk, especially if the other sensory cues are helping create a consistent virtual world.

GRAVITY

Although not quite a candidate for a seventh sense, another important sense of touch is the body's perception of the effects of gravity or g-forces. If you are driving a race car, or flying a jet plane, your body somehow knows when you are making a tight turn, or when you are flying up or down. Part of this sensation is related to the more general tactile sense, since the action of g-forces on the body results in differential pressure on the receptors on the skin. The other part is the sensation most of us have had riding a roller coaster—the sensation that your stomach has achieved existential independence, and is at that moment seeking a new home somewhere else inside your body.

Flying and driving simulators make use of the body's sense of g-forces to fool it into thinking it's going where it isn't. Tilting the driver's seat to the left (counterclockwise) produces sensations similar to those experienced when the vehicle turns right. Similarly, tilting the seat backward produces a feeling of acceleration, while tilting it forward produces a feeling of braking. G-forces are the basis for the Star Tours ride at Disneyland, which creates the sensation of movement by making the individual seats and the entire room tilt and pitch.

SMELL

If anyone ever develops a virtual reality system for dogs, you can bet that it would include an olfactory muzzle. Unlike humans, for whom odors are merely an enhancement of the total experience, dogs use their sense of smell to communicate and interact with their environment. Even so, concepts of Smellovision and Aromarama have been bandied about for years, and even actually used in a few instances.

The first use of smell in a commercially viable form was with the Sensorama device we discussed earlier, the multisensual simulator patented by Morton Heilig in 1962. Other attempts to use the sense of smell as part of the entertainment experience have bordered on the gimmicky. John Waters's 1981 cult film *Polyester*, starring Divine, was shown in Odorama. Members of the audience were given scratch 'n sniff cards, and were instructed to scratch the appropriate panels at various points in the film. The card was supposed to reproduce smells associated with dirty socks, pizza, and cheap perfume, among others. The result was campy at best.

The problem with smell in virtual reality is that it cannot be reproduced electronically. Olfaction depends on the interaction of molecular particles with the olfactory sensors in the nose. Short of direct stimulation of the brain (which is certainly outside the realur of virtual reality), the only way to create the sensation of an odor is to introduce the actual odor (or the close imitation thereof) into the nose. This would require canisters of odoriferous gases feeding, the AMD, a technique that would be cumbersome at best.

Chapter 3
Applications for Virtual
Reality Systems

Virtual reality technology has a number of real-world applications. In this chapter, we'll look at the role of cyberspace in entertainment, architecture, medicine, and technology.

ENTERTAINMENT

The entertainment industry might be thought of as means of collecting a little money from each of a lot of people. For example, it only costs a quarter or fifty cents to play a video game in an arcade, yet so many people played them in the early 1980s that the video arcade industry made more money than Hollywood. That's a lot of quarters. Likewise, it costs about seven bucks to see a movie, and if enough people see it, the movie industry makes a bundle.

It is this accumulation of large amounts of money gathered from a large number of people that allows the entertainment industry to participate in the latest advances in technology. In the movies, the progression has been from the silents, to talkies, to color, to CinemaScope, to Cinerama, to the almost-virtual experiences of Star Tours and Captain EO at Disneyland. In arcade games, it has been from the black-and-white Pong, to more sophisticated color games, to the laserdisk-based Dragon's Lair, to Sega's mirror-based Hologram game.

In both cases, the progression has been from the first primitive sputterings of the technology toward greater and greater realism. For the movies, the ultimate experience is to be an invisible spectator in a very real environment, immersed in the story and its characters. For video games, the ultimate experience is to be a seminal character immersed in the make-believe world, striving toward a difficult but attainable goal.

Figure 3.1 The Virtuality 1000 SD lets you fly or drive through various environments

Figure 3.2 *The Virtuality 1000 CS is designed for multiplayer games like Dactyl Nightmare*

CYBERSPACE ARCADES

Virtuality, the first virtual reality arcade games, are now installed in a number of video arcades in the United States. People have been forming long lines and paying four dollars to experience four minutes of cyberspace. We can expect cyberspace arcades to start appearing in all the likely places: amusement parks, shopping malls, and other locations that attract crowds of people.

The Virtuality machines are based on an Amiga 3000 CPU, with additional plug-in boards to enhance graphics and animation. The machines are upgradeable through software, allowing operators to change to a different game (or improve the current game) simply by installing new software.

The Virtuality machines come in two styles, a sit-down version and a stand-up version (see Figures 3.1 and 3.2). Both allow multiple players to share the same virtual space, and battle each other as though they were mere characters in a video game. The sit-down model is ideal for flying and driving simulations, while the stand-up model is designed for exploration on foot, or for hand-to-hand combat in multiple-player games. Virtuality machines are manufactured by W. Industries in the United Kingdom and distributed by Horizon Entertainment in the United States. See Appendix A for more information on these and other suppliers of virtual reality products.

Whatever the reason (is the real reality really so bad?), the world is ready for the next generation of video games, virtual reality machines—where you are totally involved and participate in a world that seems real but isn't.

ARCHITECTURE

Imagine a visit to the architectural office of the future. You, the client, are ushered into the board room, which contains a virtual reality system housed in a large cubicle in the corner of the room. While a technician readies the machine for the presentation, the lead architect describes the philosophy behind the design, setting the stage for the walkthrough of a building that doesn't yet exist. As soon as the machine is ready, you enter the cubicle and put on the head-mounted display and the data glove. Your free hand remains poised over four directional keys on a keypad.

You are immediately thrust into an alternate reality. You are standing in the lobby of a small hotel. Directly ahead you can see the main desk, and to your right you see the bank of elevators. You turn right and press the "Forward" key on the keypad, which propels you toward the elevators. You release the Forward button, and then reach out with your data-gloved hand to press the elevator button. Although there is no real button, you feel a sensation of pressure on your index finger, caused by the tactors imbedded in the glove.

The elevator doors open, and you step inside and turn around. You press the button for the fifth floor, and you watch the doors close and the indicator move to the first, second, and finally the fifth floor. The elevator doors open, and you step out, ready to explore the top floor of your small hotel.

This scenario is not as distant as you might think. VPL Research, Inc., which markets the MicroCosm virtual reality system, is currently developing a virtual reality walkthrough of the entire city of Berlin. "Flythrough" might be a more apt description. Instead of waiting for a ricketty old bus to take you from A to B, you will be able to put your data-gloved fingers together in a special way to fly to your destination, just like Mary Poppins did when she clicked her heels.

Two of the programs we've included with this book will give you a taste of the architectural walkthrough of the future, and you can run them both on a standard PC. Superscape, which is described as desktop virtual reality, lets you maneuver a humanoid figure or drive a car around an industrial complex. You can also fly around the complex in a helicopter.

The second program is a game created using Virtual Reality Studio, a commercial product that lets you create a virtual world, attach conditions to the occurrence of certain events, and then explore the world using a standard point-and-click interface on your PC. This game, which we call Lemme Out of Here! will both challenge and frustrate you.

MEDICINE

X-rays are not as benign as they were thought to be in the 1940s and 1950s. Movies of that era portraying X-ray technology usually showed the patient standing behind an X-ray machine while the physician watched the patient's innards pulsating in real time. That kind of exposure today would make an oncologist shudder, since the radiation from X-ray machines has been closely linked to cancer and other ills. Indeed, today patients are exposed to X-rays for periods that are measured in milliseconds, not the minutes that it would take to watch a patient swallow a barium milkshake.

These days, X-ray technology is being superseded by *magnetic resonance imaging* (MRI), a non-invasive method for looking at the inside of the human body. Using weak and harmless magnetic fields, this technology, coupled with virtual reality techniques, has given rise to a fascinating application in the field of internal medicine. Figure 3.3 diagrams this technique.

The MRI device points to a specific part of the patient's body, producing the images that are displayed on the HMD's twin monitors. As the physician moves around in the HMD, the imaging device mimics those movements, moving its sensor to the corresponding part of the patient's body and sending a stream of data to the displays. To the doctor, it seems as though she is actually looking

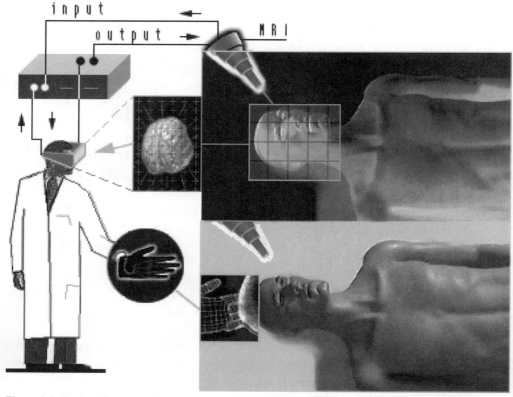

Figure 3.3 *As the physician moves her head, the computer moves the imaging device, which in turn sends a new set of signals to the head-mounted display. The effect is one of "X-ray glasses"*

through X-ray glasses at the patient. She can move her head to look at the patient's internal organ first from the front, then from the side, and finally from the back, to get a complete, continuous picture in real time and in three dimensions. And all this without even having to be in the same room as the patient.

The next step will allow a physician to go "inside" the body as a microscopic organism and explore every nook and cranny. Instead of swallowing a barium milkshake to light up your insides, you would simply sit in a comfortable chair while your physician walks around inside you.

It is every adolescent's dream to own a pair of X-ray glasses (for reasons that are certainly not relevant to this book). While it may be awhile before the HMD/MRI combination is affordable to those of us who are at the mercy of a weekly allowance, the technology has its foot in the door, and it won't be long before the rest of it follows.

TECHNOLOGY

Our human bodies would be capable of doing a lot more than we do if only we were bigger, or stronger, or better able to withstand the effects of radiation, or smaller, or thinner.

Although we are better equipped to directly manipulate our immediate environment than most other species (thanks in part to our enviable finger-thumb opposition, among other advantages), there is still a multitude of tasks that we are simply unable to undertake because of our physical limitations. For example, we cannot directly handle radioactive materials, and so we must use shielded gloves protruding into a lead-lined box. We don't have the manual dexterity (or the visual acuity) to directly move molecules around inside a compound, or the sheer physical strength to move objects weighing several tons.

Virtual reality techniques can help us overcome some of these limitations. Imagine, for example, a virtual world in which you can pick up and manipulate objects with exact precision. You watch as your virtual hand picks up a virtual object in the display and lays it carefully in a predetermined location. The action is easy and effortless on your part. Meanwhile, however, the computer is controlling a heavy-duty robotic arm that mimics your every movement, and which is picking up and manipulating objects weighing several tons apiece.

Virtual reality can also help overcome our physical limitations at the other end of the scale, by helping us manipulate objects that are too small for us to even see. So-called molecule docking uses the same virtual reality techniques as the above example, except that it deals with microscopic particles. In this case, your virtual hand reaches into cyberspace and maneuvers a virtual object into position, while the computer controls the same activity at the molecular level.

It's easy to imagine other applications for virtual reality as a form of body amplification. Undersea exploration using virtual reality techniques can allow us to go deeper and farther than ever before. Thanks to virtual reality, the human body is no longer the limiting factor in any field of endeavor—except maybe the Olympic Games. And even that exalted athletic event may one day include contests between computer-controlled robots piloted by cybernauts, just as chess tournaments today allow the participation of computers.

PART 2
VIRTUAL REALITY PLAYHOUSE

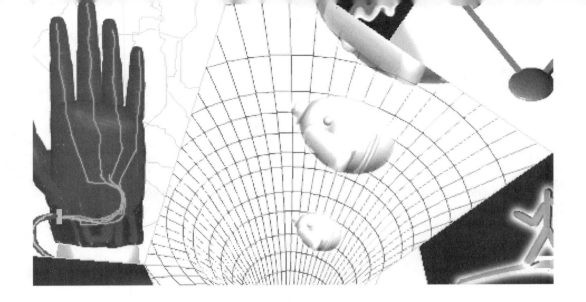

Before we begin exploring our collection of virtual reality software, let's look at where our little journey might take us. First, remember that *Virtual Reality Playhouse* is just that: a *playhouse*, and not a four-bedroom, three-bath family home with a two-car garage. While a full-fledged virtual reality system can fool you into thinking you are experiencing another reality, the software we've included in this package isn't going to fool you into thinking you are anywhere but at your desk. So unless you're running a fever and are experiencing a mild delusional system, don't expect the software in our package to transport you to any kind of alternate reality.

On the other hand, even though a playhouse is not designed as a substitute for a primary residence, it is designed to let you have fun and get an idea of what virtual reality systems are like. The software we have included here uses the same kind of technology used by the dedicated virtual reality systems, but on a much smaller scale, and without the costly peripherals described earlier. (However, we will show you how to build your own low-cost LCD shutter glasses and data gloves to use with your PC; see Appendices A and D for more information.)

So while you may not experience the total immersion experience of the bigger virtual reality systems, you will get to play with some intriguing software, and get a glimpse of the reality behind virtual reality.

SUPERSCAPE

Guide a "virtual" human around an industrial park, and experience it from his point of view. Tired of walking? Jump into one of the two cars and drive around the complex. Or fly around it in the helicopter, and see how it looks from the sky. Use the keyboard to change control, perspective, and point of view. Not only can you experience the virtual world from the viewpoint of these objects, but you can also rotate your camera in any direction and view the entire scene from any angle. You can even walk upside down, or drive a car into a room.

WIRE 3D

Put on the red-blue 3-D glasses included in your package and rotate a wireframe object that appears to float somewhere inside your monitor. We have included over twenty wireframe images that you can view in 3-D, plus detailed instructions for creating your own. We have even included the source code, so you can modify it for your own specific applications.

STARE-EO

Experience the most amazing 3-D phenomenon without 3-D glasses. This effect is more difficult to achieve, but will give you a breathtaking experience when you finally "get it." Based on the binocular fusion of random dot patterns, Stare-EO lets you paint color images on the screen, and then translates the colors into distances along the z-axis to give you a three-dimensional image.

LEMME OUT OF HERE!

Explore this extra-planetary virtual world and try to find your way back to Earth. No immersion, but plenty of navigation and manipulation. Use your mouse and the program's intuitive point-and-click interface to explore and interact with this mysterious world. We won't give away the solution, but we'll give you a few clues to get you started.

CONTINUUM

Jump from one platform to another until you reach the exit door halfway up the wall. Use your joystick or keyboard to maneuver yourself around three-space. Pick up friendly cubes and crystals along the way for extra points, but avoid the deadly forcefields and energy drains, and the other bad guys lurking about. You can modify your point of view, the camera angles, and four other display options to suit your own personal preferences (and your sense of challenge).

MIG-29 FULCRUM

This smooth flight simulator lets you pilot a MiG reconnaissance jet over land and sea. Although you won't see action with this demo version, you will get a chance to try out your flying skills on one of the fastest flight simulators around. Use your keyboard or joystick to fly around and fire missiles, rockets, or canons.

3DV

Rotate wireframe objects on the screen in real time. Choose from eleven different images, and rotate them in any direction using your mouse. No need for 3-D glasses or binocular convergence with this one. The keyword here is fast.

3DGV

This program controls the modified Sega LCD shutter glasses, so you can view 3-D images on your PC. We weren't able to include a pair of the Sega glasses with this book, but we have included instructions for modifying the glasses to work with your PC.

3DBENCH

Play a 3-D animation on your PC, and see how fast it runs.

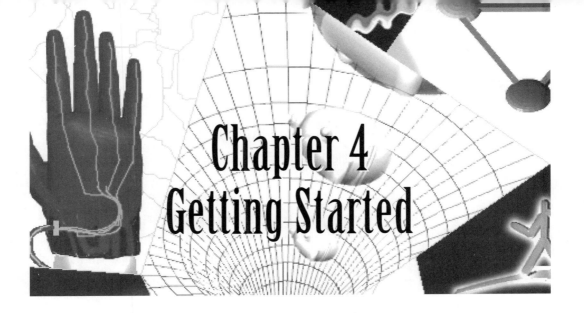

Chapter 4
Getting Started

If you are familiar with computer software, and are comfortable using MS-DOS, then you probably don't need to read every word of this chapter. You probably already know enough to jump in and at least get your feet wet. However, we do recommend you read the following general description of the software, and the section on Hardware Requirements, to make sure your system has everything you need to work with our software. After that you can explore on your own, and refer to the manual for specific information on using a particular program.

On the other hand, if you need a little help with the mysteries of DOS, or you just want to make sure that you are not missing an important step in the installation process, then it's probably a good idea to read the installation instructions as well as the section on Hardware Requirements. After you have the software installed on your hard disk (or on one or more floppies), you are then free to explore the software in any order you wish.

THE SOFTWARE

The nine programs we have included in this book are stored on the included disk in a compressed format. Before you can run any of them, you will have to decompress them, and then put the decompressed files either onto another floppy disk or onto your hard drive. We used a compression utility which creates self-extracting files. Note that a single compressed file can consist of a number of decompressed files. These files will not be evident until the file is decompressed.

Software Requirements

The only software requirement for running the programs we've included is that you are using MS-DOS 3.3 or later. If you are using an earlier version of DOS, you can obtain an upgrade though your dealer.

HARDWARE REQUIREMENTS

To run the software we've included in this book, you will need to have the following hardware *as an absolute minimum*:

- IBM AT (or compatible) computer, with at least 640K of Random Access Memory (RAM). Even though some of the programs will run on a PC level computer, you will get better results with an AT, which uses the 80286 (or just simply "286") chip as the central processing unit (CPU), and runs at clock speeds of 10 MHz to 16 MHz. More advanced CPUs based on the 386 or 486 chip and running at clock speeds of 20 to 40 MHz provide better performance, both with the software included with this book and in general.

- Color monitor driven by an EGA, VGA, MCGA, or SVGA display board. The EGA board gives your computer the capability of displaying sixteen colors at the same time. You will get more out of the software if you use a VGA or MCGA display board with a corresponding monitor. Note that some (though not all) of the programs we have included will work with the Hercules (monochrome) board and a monochrome monitor. Note also that one of the programs (the Superscape demo) requires a VGA or MCGA display.

- Two floppy drives, one of which must be a 5.25 inch drive, or one 5.25 inch floppy drive and a hard disk. If you only have 3.5 inch drives, you might ask your local computer store if they would copy the disk onto several disks of that format. A hard disk will make life easier for you (see recommendation below).

- A serial mouse.

The above is the minimum configuration needed to get you going with the software. For better results, we recommend you add the following to your system:

- A hard (or "fixed") disk. This lets you store greater amounts of data than the highest density floppy drives, and lets you access the data much faster. Running a program from a floppy disk can result in annoying delays as data is loaded from the disk.

As we mentioned earlier, the more advanced the CPU (based on a 386 or 486 chip) and the faster its clock speed, the better the performance with the software. This is particularly true of the flight simulator and the Superscape demo, where large amounts of data are continually being processed by the CPU.

By the same token, a VGA or MCGA display will give you more colors and better resolution than a lesser display. Although not critical for viewing most of this software, the more advanced displays give you superior realism. And isn't superior realism what virtual reality is all about?

INSTALLING THE SOFTWARE

You can install the software ready to run in one of two ways. If you want to look at one or two of the programs on the disk, you can decompress just those files and leave the others as they are. Or you can decompress all the files at once, and then look at them at your convenience. Whichever method you choose, you will first need to decide where to put the decompressed files, which in turn depends on whether or not you are using a hard disk.

HARD DISK USERS

If you are using a hard disk, we recommend you create a directory for the *Virtual Reality Playhouse* files, and then copy all the files from the disk into that directory. After that you can decompress the file or files you are interested in playing with, putting the decompressed file in the same directory as the original. You can then delete the compressed file to free up room on your hard disk. (Remember, you still have the original disk with the original compressed files, so you aren't really throwing anything away.)

That way, you can go straight to the appropriate directory whenever you feel like virtualizing, and load the program you want to play with. To create a directory for your *Virtual Reality Playhouse* files, first log on to the hard drive by typing:

C: (Enter)

This displays the C-prompt (C:\>). (If you have multiple hard drives, or if your hard drive has a different designation, use that designation instead of C.) Now type the following:

MD VRPLAY (Enter)

This creates a directory called VRPLAY on your hard disk. Note that if you were already in a directory when you gave that command, DOS will place your new directory inside it. In that case, to get to the VRPLAY directory, you would need to go to the "Parent" directory first.

Next you need to switch to the new directory. Type:

`CD VRPLAY` (Enter)

You are now inside the new directory (which is still empty). The next step is to copy all the files from the original floppy disk into this new directory. To do this we will use XCOPY with the /S option, which copies all the subdirectories. First, insert your original *Virtual Reality Playhouse* disk into your 5.25 inch drive (which we are assuming is designated Drive A), and then type:

`XCOPY A:\*.* /S` (Enter)

XCOPY will copy all the files and subdirectories into the VRPLAY directory on the hard disk. Note: If your floppy drive has a designation other than A, substitute the correct designation in the above command. For example, if your 5.25 inch drive is your B drive, substitute B for A in the above command. To check that everything was copied properly, type:

`DIR` (Enter)

The screen should display the following:

```
.               <DIR>
..              <DIR>
EXTRACT         BAT
README          TXT
3DBENCH         <DIR>
3DGV            <DIR>
3DGV            <DIR>
CONTIN          <DIR>
GLOVE           <DIR>
LEMME           <DIR>
MIG29           <DIR>
STAREO          <DIR>
SUPRSCAP        <DIR>
WIRE3D          <DIR>
```

(The files will not necessarily be in this order).

The next step is to decompress the files. If you want to decompress all the files at once, you can use the batch (EXTRACT.BAT) file we created for this purpose. The batch file will decompress each compressed file, put the new files in the appropriate directory, and then delete the original compressed file from your hard disk. To run the batch file, type:

`EXTRACT.BAT` (Enter)

If you prefer, you can decompress the compressed files one at a time, manually. Use the following instructions to decompress individual files, beginning with 3DV. Of course, you can decompress them in any order you wish, so just use the following instructions as a guideline.

First, switch to the 3DV directory by typing:

`CD 3DV` (Enter)

Next, to decompress the 3DV file type:

`X3DV` (Enter)

This decompresses all the files contained in the compressed file and puts them in the 3DV directory. To check that everything went smoothly, type:

`DIR` (Enter)

You should see the following directory on the screen:

```
3DV         ZIP
2SKULLS     3D
3DV         DOC
3DV         EXE
CONVERT     TXT
DATA        3DV
GALAXY      3D
GLASS       3D
HEIGHTS     3D
HOUSE       3DV
SHUTTLE     3DV
SKULL       3D
SOLIDS      3D
SURFACE     3D
TREE1       3DV
```

Now that 3DV files have been decompressed, you can delete the original compressed file and free up some room on your hard disk. To do so, type:

`3DV.EXE` (Enter)

If you can't wait to run the 3DV demo, turn to the 3DV part of the book and follow the instructions there. Or you can go ahead and decompress the remaining files. Because the commands are the same in each case, we'll just give you one more example. After that you're on your own. Just remember to switch to the appropriate directory each time.

To decompress the 3DGV files, first switch to the 3DGV directory by typing

`CD..` (Enter)

and then

`CD 3DGV` (Enter)

to get into the 3DGV directory.

To decompress the 3DGV files, type:

3DGV (Enter)

Once you have decompressed the file or files you want to use, you can turn to the instructions for using the *Virtual Reality Playhouse* demos. Each program has its own set of instructions, which you can find under the Up and Running heading in that program's section of the book.

Floppy Drive Users

If you are using *Virtual Reality Playhouse* with floppy drives only, you will have to put the decompressed files onto one or more floppy disks. Because not all the files will fit onto a single floppy, you will have to decompress the files one at a time.

Your strategy will be to decompress as many of the demo programs as will fit onto a single blank disk (which we refer to as your "work" disk). Then you will need to insert a new blank disk into the target drive (so-called because it is the "target" of the decompressed files).

Note that the following commands assume that you put your original 5.25 inch disk in Drive A, and your work disk in Drive B. If your drives have a different designation, substitute the appropriate letters in the following commands. For example, if your original disk is in Drive B and the blank disk is in Drive A, just switch A and B in the commands.

To decompress the 3DV files, insert your original disk in Drive A, and a blank (formatted) disk in Drive B. First, switch to Drive A, by typing:

A: (Enter)

To decompress the 3DV files, for instance, and put them onto the disk in Drive B, type:

CD 3DV (Enter)

This will put you in the correct directory. Then type:

X3DV B: (Enter)

The compression utility will decompress the file and put it onto your blank disk. You can now run the decompressed file, or you can decompress another. You can decompress all the files using the same instruction, changing only the filename each time.

Once you have decompressed the file or files you want to use, you can then go to the instructions for using the *Virtual Reality Playhouse* files. Each program has its own set of instructions, following the Up and Running heading in that program's section of the book.

RUNNING 3D-BENCH

To make sure that everything went OK, we'll end this installation section by running a simple demo program that also doubles as a benchmark test of your computer.

  This self-running demo was created using the virtual reality creation software from Dimension International, the developers who provided the Superscape demo. The demo serves as a benchmark test of your computer by letting you know the frame rate of the animation it displays. Faster computers will display a rate of 15 frames/sec or more.

  To see the 3DBench demo, first go to the 3DBENCH subdirectory, and then type:

3DBENCH (Enter)

  Then just settle back and watch the animation. To quit the demo and return to DOS, press Esc at any time.

Chapter 5
Superscape:
Desktop Virtual Reality

Here is a virtual world you can explore from several points of view. You can explore the industrial park through the eyes of a human on foot, or you can drive around it in either of two cars. You can even fly around the complex in a helicopter. As the "virtual human," you can walk into an office and explore its spartan furnishings. Before we begin, however, let's look at the philosophy behind this demonstration.

At first sight, the concept of "desktop virtual reality" might seem like a contradiction in terms. If virtual reality involves immersion, navigation, and manipulation (as we saw earlier), with its attendant array of complex and expensive hardware, how can a mere desktop system, no matter how powerful, fool you into thinking you are a different world? The short answer is that it doesn't. Desktop virtual reality is virtual reality without the immersion, which means that you are not going to be fooled into thinking you are "in" another world, and you are not going to fall out of your chair reaching for the virtual brass ring while riding the virtual carousel.

Nonetheless, desktop virtual reality does retain much of the navigation and manipulation of the "real" virtual reality systems, giving you the ability to move around the virtual world, rotate your camera view to see things from impossible angles, and manipulate its components. And although such a scaled down non-head-mounted display, non-glove, non-immersive virtual reality system may lack the totality of the experience afforded by the bigger systems, it does make the technology available to a wider audience. To use a weak analogy, just because movies are best viewed on a big screen with multichannel THX sound, doesn't mean one can't enjoy watching movies on TV.

UP AND RUNNING

Before you start the demo, make sure your mouse driver is already installed if you want to use the mouse for navigation. If you haven't unzipped the compressed file, you will need to do that before you can continue. Refer to Installing the Software earlier, for specific instructions. When you are ready to start, switch to the SUPRSCAP directory (or to the disk containing the Superscape files), and type:

DEMO (Enter)

In a few moments, you will see a startup screen, followed by a text screen providing information about the Superscape developers. At this point, you can press any key to enter the Superscape virtual world (see Figure 5.1).

Press I to bring up an information screen summarizing the keyboard commands, and then go ahead and explore on your own, navigating about the virtual world on your screen. If you need more detailed instructions for running the demo, you can turn to the following section for help.

Figure 5.1 The Superscape industrial park

USING THE SOFTWARE

Superscape's keyboard commands fall into three main categories: Viewpoint options and controls, Object Control options and keys, and miscellaneous keys.

Viewpoint options and control keys affect what you see of the industrial park, as though you are moving a camera around. You can navigate around the complex from a number of different viewpoints, such as an outside view, an inside view of the office, or an overhead view of the entire park.

Superscape starts out with the outside viewpoint (see Figure 5.1, earlier), with the camera behind and a little to the right of the human figure. You can always return to that viewpoint at any time by pressing F1. To view the complex from the same viewpoint but from a lower vantage point (as though you had sat down on the ground, for example), press F2. Superscape gives you two additional viewpoints: press F3 for a view of the inside of the office (see Figure 5.2), and F4 for an overhead view of the entire complex (see Figure 5.3). Remember that these are just viewpoints, and are not necessarily related to the object currently under your control. For example, if you are controlling the human figure from the outside viewpoint (F1), pressing F3 to view the inside of the office will not automatically place the human figure there.

Figure 5.2 *Interior of Superscape office*

Figure 5.3 *Overhead view of entire complex*

Object Control options and movement keys let you control the various objects in the industrial park, such as the human figure, the red or blue cars, or the helicopter flying overhead. You can attach the camera to each of these objects, to see things from different viewpoints.

Superscape lets you control all four of the objects in the industrial park, simultaneously if you wish. Once you relinquish control of an object (by attaining control over one of the others), the first object will continue along the same path until it encounters an obstacle. You can jump around from object to object, intoxicated with your newly acquired power. Note that you can control the red car from two different viewpoints. Press F6 to control the red car from the driver's seat (see Figure 5.4) or F7 to control from outside (see Figure 5.5).

A complete list of the Object Control keys is given on page 62.

Miscellaneous keys let you modify some of the settings in the software, such as turning the horizon on and off, zooming in or zooming out, and increasing or decreasing the level of detail in the image. Refer to the complete list of Miscellaneous keys on page 62-63.

Figure 5.4 *In the driver's seat of the red car*

A GUIDED TOUR

We'll explore the Superscape demo with a short guided tour, so that you can get some experience with its many functions and features. After that, you're on your own, free to explore the industrial park in any way you see fit. In this guided tour, we'll maneuver our human figure (let's call him "Soupie") over to the Superscape office and turn on the computer. Note that you can press the Backspace key at any time to pause the demo. Press any key to restart.

Start by pressing F10 to reset all objects to their original positions and states. Next press F5 to control Soupie, and then the Up Arrow key (or Kpad 8) to move him forward. You can make Soupie go faster by pressing the Up Arrow key, and you can slow him down by pressing the Down Arrow key. Each press increases (or decreases) Soupie's speed by a factor.

Once you get Soupie going at a comfortable clip, keep him moving forward until you reach the end of the main road. Cross the street at the end of the first block, and keep going until you reach the end of the second block. Cross that street and then turn right by pressing the Right Arrow (or Kpad 6)

Figure 5.5 *Outside view of red car*

key repeatedly until you are perpendicular to your original direction. Soupie will continue moving forward, so you won't need to press the Up Arrow key again, unless you want to speed him up.

Next we will go to the end of this block and then turn left to reach the entrance to the office. Incidentally, the building is the Superscape building; you can see its logo at the top near the roof.

You should continually look out for the red car that is driving around the block. This car has been observed driving on the sidewalk, so you should exercise a little care. If the car should come within striking distance of Soupie (or of the other car, for that matter), all forward activity will just stop until you can maneuver the objects out of the jam. (Sorry, but there aren't any spectacular collisions in this demo). When Soupie is up against an obstacle, he can only move one step at a time.

You may want to press F4 at this point, for a bird's-eye view of the complex. This will help you keep track of the red car and its erratic driver. Press F5 to return to the previous view.

Once you get to the end of this block, turn left by pressing the Left Arrow key. Now as you maneuver Soupie toward the office door, you can look into the office through the transparent window on Soupie's left. The office door is just beyond the first window. Turn Soupie left until he is facing the office door, and then let him move forward and through the door. (Just as it should in any modern office complex, the door opens automatically as Soupie approaches it.)

Once you are in the office, you can guide Soupie around to the computer. To zoom in to the computer, press the > key repeatedly. The computer will get closer and closer, until you see a switch on the left side of the monitor. Click the switch with the left mouse button to turn the computer on; click it again to turn it off.

You may have already guessed what the Radiation readout at the lower left part of the screen is all about. This simply indicates how close you are to the radioactive box on the desk in the office. If you zoom in on the box, you will notice that it carries the international symbol for radioactivity. Click the box, and it's gone. The radiation level now drops below 10 (it was hovering around 200 as you zeroed in on it).

Clicking the box made it disappear from the office, but it is now somewhere else in the complex. Your next job is to find out exactly where it is and click it again. (Hint: You may want to poke around the big sign at the entrance to the complex.)

Well, that's just about a full day's work for our friend Soupie. If you want to explore further, we'll hand over the controls to you. Refer to Tables 5.1, 5.2, and 5.3 for additional controls. Remember, if you get stuck, you can always go back to Square One by pressing F10.

F1	Outside viewpoint, looking into the complex
F2	Outside viewpoint, from a lower vantage point
F3	Inside view of office
F4	Overhead view of complex

Once you have established your viewpoint, you can use the following keys to change your viewing direction:

Q	Look left
W	Look right
N	Tilt view left
M	Tilt view right
P	Look up
L	Look down
Kpad 7	Face forward (also Home key)
U	U-turn

Use the following keys to move your viewpoint forward, backward, or sideways:

O	Move view forward
K	Move view backward
H	Move view left
J	Move view right
R	Move view up
F	Move view down

Use the following keys to select the object to control:

F5	Control human figure (rear, overhead view)
F6	Control red car (view from inside car)
F7	Control red car (overhead view)
F8	Control blue car (rear, overhead view)
F9	Control helicopter (side view)

Table 5.1 Viewpoint keys

Once you have selected the object, use the following keys for specific controls:

Kpad 8	Accelerate object (also Up Arrow)
Kpad 2	Decelerate object (also Down Arrow)
Kpad 4	Turn object left (also Left Arrow)
Kpad 6	Turn object right (also Right Arrow)
Kpad -	Move object up
Kpad +	Move object down
Kpad 9	Pitch object up
Kpad 3	Pitch object down
Kpad 0	Stop object (also Insert)
A	Reenable auto route (red car)

Table 5.2 Object Control keys

Use the following keys to make miscellaneous global changes to the software:

F10	Reset all objects to their original (default) positions
I	Display Information screen
D	Cycle through four levels of detail (for faster performance)
B	Toggle horizon On/Off (for faster performance)
V	Toggle mouse On/Off
S	Change step size for viewpoint movement

T	Change step size for turning
>	Zoom In
<	Zoom Out
X	Lock X rotation On/Off (when controlling object)
Y	Lock Y rotation On/Off (when controlling object)
Z	Lock Z rotation On/Off (when controlling object)
Backspace	Pause demo (press any key to restart)
Shift F1 - F9	Save the current viewpoint and any controlled object to the specified function key
Esc	Exit to DOS

Table 5.3 *Miscellaneous keys*

Some of these controls can get pretty technical. For example, you can use the X, Y, and Z keys to lock and unlock the corresponding axis for the object under control. Say you are controlling the red car from above (F7) and you press the Right Arrow, (or Kpad 6). In that case, the car turns right (or actually rotates about the y-axis, the axis that runs perpendicular to the horizon), as you observe from a fixed point of view. In other words, the car rotates on the screen, while the complex remains fixed as your point of reference. Pressing Y locks the y-axis for the red car and changes your point of reference to the car. Now when you press the Right Arrow, the car remains fixed on the screen while the complex rotates around it. Think of the point of reference as a camera. In one case, the camera is fixed to the object, and in the other, it is fixed to the complex. The same applies to the x- and z-axes, and to the other objects you can control, including Soupie and the helicopter.

To activate an object, place the mouse pointer over the object and click the left mouse button (or press Kpad *). The following are some of the things you can activate:

- Soupie's head and legs

- radioactive source (on desk in office)

- computer in office

- office doors and chair

The essence of the Superscape demo is exploration. Feel free to wander around the industrial park and try out different things. Try navigating around in the red or the blue car, or in the helicopter. Go into the office and try moving the chairs around. Imagine that you are the client of a firm of architects, and that you have just been handed the design for your industrial park on a disk.

A WINDOW INTO ANOTHER DIMENSION

Dimension International, the distributor of SuperScape, manufactures a class of high-end virtual reality products. These include Desktop VR™, a turnkey virtual reality system consisting of hardware (a 486/33 based PC enhanced with special graphics processors), software (Superscape Visualiser, which was used to create the SuperScape demo, and an innovative input device (the Spaceball 2003 6-axis controller). See Figure 5.6 for a look at Dimension International's enhanced 486 PC and the Spaceball controller.

Figure 5.6 Virtual reality hardware distributed by Dimension International includes an enhanced 486 PC and a 6-axis Spaceball controller

SUPERSCOOP

Ian Andrew, Dimension International's Director of Marketing, answered a few questions for programmers:

Q. Please describe your product for making Virtual Worlds.

A. This is called the Virtual Reality Toolkit. There are four parts:

1. The Visualiser for real time visualization and interaction including several example worlds,

2. the Shape Editor—a real time solid 3-D shape modeler (as shown in Figure 5.7)

3. the World Editor—a real time virtual creation utility, (as shown in Figure 5.8) and

4. libraries of ready made shapes and objects.

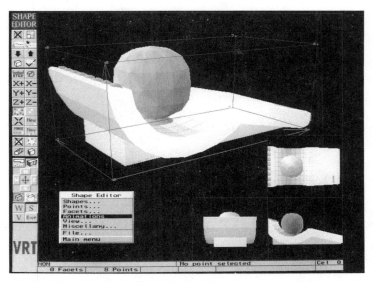

Figure 5.7 *The Virtual Reality Toolkit's Shape Editor allows you to design complex, solid, 3D shapes such as a Spaceball controller*

This utility also provides for assigning physical properties to objects, i.e.. velocities, rotational velocities, effects under gravity, friction animation's and even the facility to assign conditional instructions to objects using an inbuilt 400 word language—SCL (Superscape Control Language).

Q. What is the Superscape language and what are its features compared to other languages such as BASIC and C?

A. The Superscape Control Language (SCL) is a language whose syntax is based on C. It is compiled to intermediate code which is compact and fast, as opposed to BASIC, where the source code itself is interpreted, or C where actual machine code instructions are generated. This allows a balance between speed and portability across different platforms.

Each object in the world may have its own SCL program. These are all executed in parallel, and each one may continue over several frames.

SCL has many of the familiar C control structures, such as if...else, do...until, while, and switch,

Figure 5.8 The World Editor lets you design complete worlds; in this case, an office

along with some of its own. It supports 32 bit integer arithmetic, along with a fast fixed-point format for handling fractions. Floating point support is being included in later versions. Arrays and pointers are also allowed, making the manipulation of tables of data very easy.

It has several hundred built-in functions specifically for controlling all aspects of the Virtual World. These include moving and rotating objects, changing colors and palettes, and checking for activation's and collisions. Users can program their own procedures, which are then called like any of the built-in ones.

One major difference with almost every language now available is that the SCL source code is not stored. When you need to edit an SCL program, the source code is "decompiled" from the compact object code and presented to you for editing. This makes program storage very memory-efficient, in keeping with the rest of the Superscape system.

Q. What are the programming constraints of working in Virtual World languages? In other words, do they require a lot of floating point calculations, are special video boards required, etc.?

A. The main system that displays the Virtual World, the Superscape system, is very processor-intensive and requires an intelligent video board to run at full speed.

SCL, however, is interested only in manipulating objects within the virtual world, so the processing required is relatively minor compared with the main job of displaying the world in real time.

These are considerations that need to be addressed when writing SCL programs, but these are mainly down to the design of how the various objects are effectively running simultaneously, synchronization of the actions on different objects is perhaps the most important consideration to be borne in mind. A built-in message passing system has been included to make this task easier (any object can send a message to any other object which can then take appropriate action depending on the content of the message).

Q. What are the specs of any special boards needed for your system and do you think one day it will work with standard SVGA hardware?

A. Our software will in the future work with standard SVGA hardware but today in order to obtain extra speed and detail we recommend a Tiga board based around the Texas 34020 chip—the best card we have found to date is the SPEA FGA4 card.

Q. Does your product work with helmet mounted displays or gloves. If not why not?

A. 1. Our Virtual Reality software, Superscape, is aimed directly at providing 3-D visualization on Desktop computers. This allows for the real time interactive 3-D visualization of Virtual Worlds without many of the limitations still associated with immersion systems.

2. The Virtual Reality Toolkit, being a virtual world creation package, generates worlds that run on both desktop and immersion systems.

Q. What kind of companies are using your product and what are they doing with it?

A. The two complimentary products—Desktop VR and the Virtual Reality Toolkit. At the present time, the majority of our users are still in the fairly early stages of building their virtual worlds and realizing the full potential of the systems. Selected clients, however, reveal an interesting cross-section of market areas and applications:

- A company working in the rapidly developing area of computerized warehousing (who wish to remain anonymous at this early stage in the project), is using Desktop VR to win new business. Desktop VR provides the company with an interactive sales presentation, focusing on the visualization of the latest techniques in warehousing systems.

- ARRL (Advanced Robotic Research Limited) is using Desktop VR as a design aid for real time visualization/simulation of hazardous environments.

- West Denton High School in Newcastle upon Tyne is using Desktop VR as a training aid. A' level students are undertaking a range of projects relating to health and safety, foreign language education and arts awareness.

- British Telecom's research center is studying Desktop VR in relation to its potential use a visualization system for telecommunications traffic analysis Network diagrams are complex and a visualization system offers a means of easily traversing layered communications structures.

FOR MORE INFO

Superscape is a demo program made available by Dimension International, the creators of software for virtual reality products. These products include Desktop VR™, a turnkey virtual reality system consisting of hardware (a 486/33 based PC enhanced with special graphics processors), software (Superscape Visualiser, which was used to create the Superscape demo), and an innovative input device (the Spaceball 2003 6-axis controller). Depending on current exchange rates, the system retails in the neighborhood of $15,000 to $20,000 US.

Dimension International
Zephyr One, Calleva Park
Aldermaston, Berkshire, RG7 4QW
Int Tel: 44 734 810077; Int fax: 44 734 816940

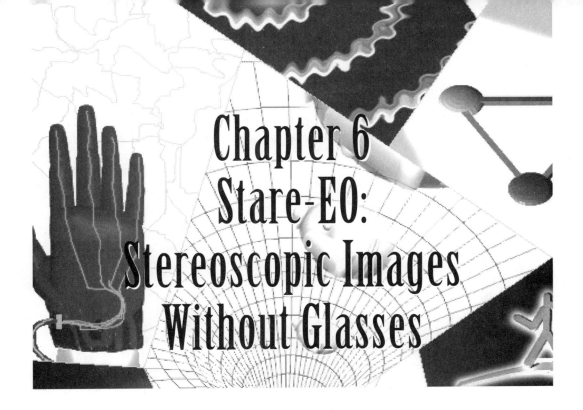

Chapter 6
Stare-EO:
Stereoscopic Images
Without Glasses

This little program is a fascinating demonstration of stereoscopic imagery without 3-D glasses. It is based on the random dot patterns sometimes referred to as Julesz figures, named after Bela Julesz, the researcher who first reported them in 1971. The Stare-EO demo does not have all the functionality of the commercial product (which we describe below), but it does give you a peek at this amazing phenomenon.

Stare-EO is a graphics program that lets you create images using all three dimensions. You paint in the *x*- and *y*-axes in the normal way, by clicking and dragging the mouse to create the shapes and lines that make up your image. Painting along the *z*-axis is accomplished by using colors as indicators of depth, color-coding the height or depth along that dimension.

For example, Stare-EO's default palette uses black for the midpoint of the *z*-axis (coinciding with the surface of the monitor), with gray as the closest point to the observer (protruding out of the monitor), and blue as the farthest point from the observer. Thus, if you were to create an image using these three shades, the blue parts of the image would appear farther away, while those colored gray would be the closest points (see Figure 6.1).

Stare-EO's EGA-compatible palette has a total of sixteen shades, providing a total of sixteen positions along the *z*-axis. Stare-EO also lets you configure the software to your personal preferences, letting you remap the colors signifying distance along the *z*-axis, or increase the depth differences between adjoining colors.

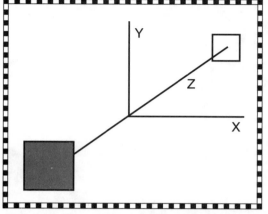

Figure 6.1 *Although you are painting on a two-dimensional surface, Stare-EO's color coding translates colors into distances along the z-axis*

When you have finished creating your image, Stare-EO converts it into a random dot pattern that gives you a 3-D image without the need for glasses. You can view the image directly on the screen, or you can print it out on a black-and-white printer. We have reproduced three Stare-EO images a little later in the book. If you are already familiar with this kind of image, you should feel free to try your hand (or eye, to be more exact) at them right away. If not, you may want to read the following sections to set the stage for this fascinating phenomenon.

As we mentioned earlier, the Stare-EO demo included on the disk does not have all the functionality of the commercial version, but it does let you create images using two depths (instead of sixteen) for viewing onscreen. The rest of the demo shows you the steps involved in the creating of a Stare-EO image, and all you have to do is sit back and watch.

A LITTLE BACKGROUND

In the earlier section on 3-D vision, we explained how when we look at an object in the real world, the retina of each eye registers a slightly different image. These two images are then fused by the brain, creating the perception of a solid object. We also explained how the anaglyphic technique of stereoscopic imagery projects a different image onto each retina by the use of red and blue lenses on 3-D glasses. Under that technique, the eye looking through the red lens sees only the blue part of the red and blue image, while the eye looking through the blue lens sees only the red part of the image.

What we didn't explain is that it is sometimes possible to achieve the same stereoscopic effect without the use of 3-D glasses, by using a technique we can call *binocular divergence*. The technique is simple in theory, even though not everybody is capable of experiencing the effect. (Roughly 10 percent of the population is incapable of experiencing the 3-D effect through the use of 3-D glasses, and a slightly larger percentage is incapable of experiencing a Julesz figure.) One reason is that the phenomenon takes a little practice to achieve—very few observers are able to see it right away. Nonetheless, it's worthwhile persevering, for the effect is so stunning when you finally see it that it will truly surprise you. The following techniques are suggestions for limbering up your eyes, getting them used to diverging (turning outward) as you stare at an object. If you feel you can already do this, you can skip the following section and go straight to the Julesz figures reproduced below. You can always come back and read this section if you are not immediately successful.

THE PHANTOM FINGER

You may remember this one from when you were growing up. It's easy to do, and uses the exact same muscular activity as the Stare-EO demo.

Place your two forefingers together, tip to tip, and hold them about 10 inches from your face. If you look at them directly, you will (we hope) see your two fingers in front of you. Nothing unusual so far (see Figure 6.2).

Now focus your eyes slightly behind your two fingers (about 10 inches again) by looking at another object, while keeping your fingers in

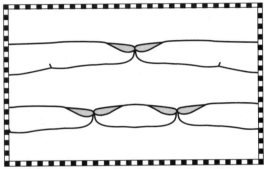

Figure 6.2 (top) You see nothing unusual when your eyes converge on two fingers touching tip to tip
Figure 6.3 (bottom) The Phantom Finger

your field of vision. If you now look at your fingers again (*without refocusing your eyes*), you will see a mysterious phantom finger between your two fingers. And if you move your fingers apart slightly, this mysterious phantom finger will appear to be suspended in space, disembodied and apparently unconnected to anything (see Figure 6.3).

What you've experienced is nothing more than the phenomenon of "seeing double" by making your eyes diverge or turn outward. Because your eyes are not converging toward the object you are looking at (in this case, your fingers), you see two images of the same object. The phantom finger is actually two of these double images overlapping each other, creating the effect of a solid but disembodied finger. Practice diverging your eyes by looking at your two fingers, and then making the phantom finger appear. This is exactly what you need to do to see the random-dot figure in the Stare-EO demo.

BEHIND THE LOOKING GLASS

Another everyday event that illustrates the same phenomenon is that of simply looking in the mirror. Whenever you look at your reflection in the mirror, your eyes are not focusing on the plane of the mirror, but rather on a plane somewhere behind the mirror. To be more exact, your eyes are

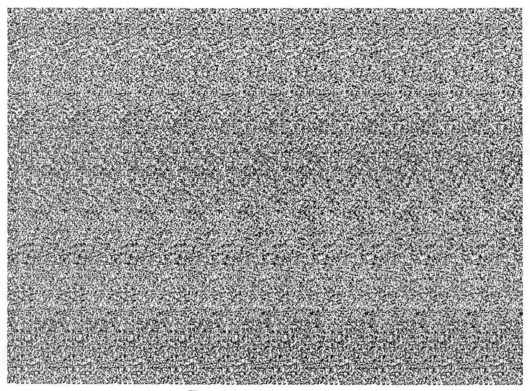

Figure 6.4 *First Stare-EO image*

focusing on a plane that is the same distance behind the mirror as you are in front of it. You can practice the same muscular movements by putting a mark on the surface of the mirror and then alternately focusing on that mark and on your reflection. When you feel that this convergence and divergence has become natural, you will be ready to try the random dot figures we have reproduced below.

THE IMAGES, ALREADY

As we mentioned earlier, it takes a little persistence to see this phenomenon, but once you see it, you will agree it was worth the effort. Let's try one (see Figure 6.4).

First, note the two black "boxes" at the top of the image. These boxes are your reference points, giving you immediate feedback on the degree of divergence of your eyes. Begin by staring at the two boxes, and then let your eyes diverge until you see three boxes. The third box (the one in the middle) is just like the phantom finger we saw earlier, and is caused by the overlapping double images.

Once you can see the third box in the middle, shift your gaze downward (*without refocusing your eyes*) and stare at the mass of random dots. In a short while you should see the image form that looks like six golf balls arranged in a circle with sides touching, at the center of the figure. The "ground" that the golf balls are resting on is made up of a set of circular ledges that converge at the center of the circle made by the golf balls. Depth wise that center is about a foot behind the figure. If you don't see it right away, keep trying. You may need to glance back at the boxes from time to time to make sure you can still see three of them. Just remember that the boxes are there to give you feedback about the degree of divergence of your eyes. The trick is to maintain that same degree of divergence as you shift your gaze down to the random dot image.

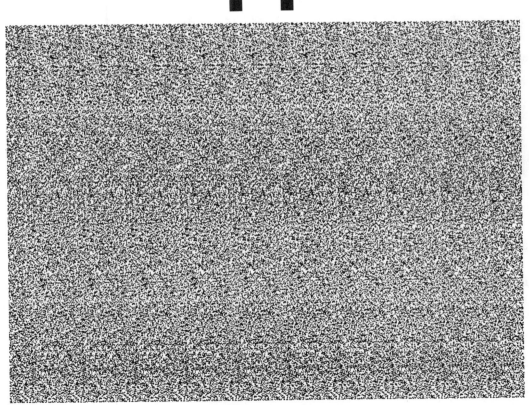

Figure 6.5 *Second Stare-EO image*

Figure 6.6 Third Stare-EO Image

The Stare-EO in Figure 6.5 appears as 15 rings standing on their sides and arranged so that there are three rows each with five rings.

The Stare-EO in Figure 6.6 is the hardest to resolve. It is made up of circular ledges that converge in the center of the page. Centered on the page are the letters "Stare EOs."

UP AND RUNNING

To use the Stare-EO demo, make sure you are in the proper directory (or the disk containing the file is in the current drive), and type:

`STW_DEMO` (Enter)

In a few moments you will see the main startup screen. Press any key to continue with the demo. Next you will see a text screen, giving you some background information about the software. At this point you can press Esc to start the demo, or Enter to go to the next page of the information screen. Pressing Esc displays the Main Menu, from which you can choose to go straight to one of the three demos, or to other information screens. These Main Menu options are described in greater detail later.

USING THE SOFTWARE

If you are itching to view the Stare-EO demo, you can just double-click the Drawing Demo #1 menu item to get it started. If you don't have a mouse, you can move the highlight bar down to the same menu item using the Up and Down Arrow keys, and then press Enter to complete the transaction. The Stare-EO demo is self-running, which means that once you get it started you can just sit back and watch it go through its paces. Stare-EO consists of three separate demos, each one producing a printable random dot pattern. If you wish, you can fast-forward through the demo by holding down both Shift keys at the same time.

The demo will pause on its second menu screen, giving you the option of No Output (the default), or output to the printer of your choice. If you just want to see the random dot image on the screen, press Enter or click Okay when the demo pauses at that menu. On the other hand, if you want to print one of the random dot patterns, you will need to specify your printer type from the scrolling list at the bottom of the menu. If you don't see your printer on the list, click the Down Arrow (or press the Down Arrow key) to scroll down the list. When your printer is highlighted, press Enter to go back to the demo.

At this point, you can just sit back and watch Stare-EO fashion a 3-D image on the screen, using its color palette to create levels of depth along the z-axis. When it has finished creating the image, Stare-EO then converts it into the random dot images reproduced above. If you like, you can try viewing the 3-D image directly on the screen, using the same technique we described earlier.

When the first demo is finished, you can try Drawing Demo #2, and then Drawing Demo #3. Of course, you are always free to explore any other part of this demo program. For example, you may want to try your hand at creating your own images. MicroSynectic, the developers of the Stare-EO program have created a version especially for *Virtual Reality Playhouse*. This special version allows you to create two-level images for viewing on the screen. See Start a New Drawing, below, for more information.

MAIN MENU OPTIONS

The following are the Main Menu options:

- *About this Demo Program:* Displays a text screen giving you general information about the Stare-EO demo.

- *Intro to Stare-EO Workshop:* Displays a text screen with information about the Stare-EO program.

- *Ordering Stare-EO Workshop:* Information screen and order form for ordering the Stare-EO program.

- *How to See Stare-EOs:* Another text screen, this time with tips for achieving the Stare-EO effect.

- *General Set Up:* Displays a text screen, followed by a secondary menu with options for modifying the default conditions. Most of the options in the secondary menu are not available in this demo version, but they will give you a good idea of the versatility of the product.

- *Drawing Demo #1:* Launches the first demo, creating the first image onscreen as you watch.

- *Drawing Demo #2:* The second demo.

- *Drawing Demo #3:* The third demo.

- *Start a New Drawing:* Brings up the main painting screen, where you can create your own two-level image for viewing on the screen. Figure 6.7 is a brief summary of the commands you can use to create your own images.

Even though the special *Virtual Reality Playhouse* demo does not let you print or save the images you create, it does let you preview them on the screen. To preview an image, press F10. This transforms your original drawing into a pattern of random dots with two levels of depth along the z-axis.

- *Import a PCX file:* Displays a text screen, explaining the procedure for importing a PC Paintbrush file into Stare-EO and creating a random dot pattern.

- *Print a File:* Lets you print one of the three demos. You will need to specify the printer you are using.

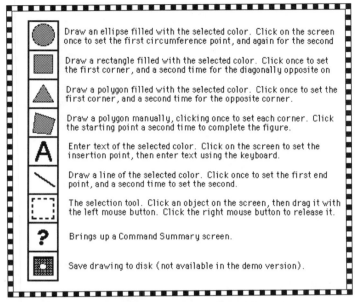

Figure 6.7 *Command summary for the Stare-EO painting screen*

- *Quit:* We should hardly have to tell you what this does. Takes you back to DOS where you can try one of the other programs in your *Virtual Reality Playhouse* directory.

If you have learned how to see the random dot stereograms, you can get the same effect by looking at the random dots on the screen. There's always the danger that someone may catch you staring at a bunch of random dots on the screen and making strange noises, so it's probably best to do this in private.

FOR MORE INFO

The Stare-EO demo was provided by NE Thing Enterprises, the publisher of the commercial product. The product, called simply Stare-EO, is available directly from NE Thing by mail order using the order form included with the demo. You can reach NE Thing at:

NE Thing Enterprises
19A Crosby Drive
Bedford, MA 01730
(617) 577-1101

Chapter 7
Lemme Out of Here!

Virtual Reality Studio is a commercial product that lets you create virtual worlds you or your friends can explore. These worlds can range from the painfully simple (such as a box shape with a door) to the excruciatingly frustrating (such as the one we have included in this book). This game (which we call Lemme Out of Here! for reasons which will soon become obvious) takes place on a distant planet. The object of the game is to find a way off the planet and back to Earth. This is easier said than done.

Let's take a look.

UP AND RUNNING

To play Lemme Out of Here!, make sure you are in the LEMME directory (or the disk containing the file is in the current drive), and type:

`RUNVGA DEMO.RUN`

The first screen asks you to select an input device (mouse, keyboard, or joystick. Make your choice by pressing the appropriate key. In a few moments, you will see the following screen (see Figure 7.1).

This game doesn't require much documentation, since most of the navigation and manipulation is by means of the control panel at the lower part of the screen. The game is best played with a mouse, although it is possible to play it with a keyboard or joystick. The following instructions are for those playing with a mouse. Specific instructions for joystick and keyboard users are given at the end of that section.

All the action takes place through your eyes, just as it should in a virtual reality game. As you move forward, the environment scrolls by you to your left and right. You can also turn left or right, and look up or down. You can shoot at things on the screen, and you can pick up or otherwise manipulate objects in your immediate environment. Here's how:

Figure 7.1 *Lemme Out of Here! main screen*

MOVING AROUND

To move in a forward direction, point to the Up Arrow at the lower right part of the Control Panel and press the left mouse button. Release the button to stop. (If you don't have the game up on the screen, you can refer to the screen shot above.) To turn to the right, press the Right Turn arrow. This will cause you to spin in a clockwise direction without actually moving away. The same applies to the Left Turn arrow, which causes you to spin in a counterclockwise direction.

The lower three arrows cause you to move to the left (perpendicular to your line of sight), to move backward, and to move to the right. These six arrows control your movement around the virtual world. With a little practice you will become adept enough to keep the mouse button held down, and just move the pointer from arrow to arrow.

JUST LOOKING

The arrows to the right of these six control what you see, but without affecting your movement. The Up Arrow causes you to look upward. If you hold the button down, your field of vision will go full circle and return to the forward view. Likewise with the Down Arrow. The Eye icon between the two arrows takes you back to the forward view.

Accumulating Things

Clicking the box to the left of the six arrows (labeled "Studio Game") displays a list of the objects you are carrying. You start this game with nothing, and you pick things up along the way. To pick up an object, you point to it on the screen, and click the right mouse button. The next time you take inventory, you will find the new object on the list.

Interacting with Objects

You also use the right mouse button to interact with objects, such as doors, or the mysterious pyramids on the roof of the first building. For example, to open a door, move the cursor to the doorknob and press the right mouse button. The door will open, and you can go on your adventurous way.

Shooting at Things

You may find it necessary to shoot at things from time to time. Sometimes this will be necessary to overcome an enemy, and other times to simply affect an object from a distance. To shoot at something, point to it and press the left mouse button.

That's all you need to know about navigating and manipulating in this virtual world. Table 7.1 shows some additional keyboard commands to give you a little more control:

Tab	Toggle between Fast and Slow game
R	Raise Vantage Point
F	Lower Vantage Point
C	Turn Center Cosshairs On/Off
N	Tilt Right (Clockwise)
M	Tilt Left (Counterclockwise)
Shift-Esc	Quit Game and Return to DOS

Table 7.1 Additional keyboard commands

Joystick and Keyboard Users

You can also play Lemme Out of Here! with the keyboard or joystick. Table 7.2 summarizes the keyboard commands. Note that these commands are also available if you are playing with a mouse or joystick, so you can actually play the game with both hands.

Q	Turn Left
W	Turn Right
H	Pan Left
J	Pan Right
A	Activate (Pick Up, Manipulate)
C	Turn Center Cosshairs On/Off
N	Tilt Right (Clockwise)
M	Tilt Left (Counterclockwise)
O	Move Forward
K	Move Back
I	Reset View
R	Raise Vantage Point
F	Lower Vantage Point
P	Rotate View Upward
L	Rotate View Down
Keypad	Move in Large Steps in Corresponding Direction
Arrows	Move in Small Steps in Corresponding Direction
Spacebar	Shoot
Shift-Esc	Quit Game and Return to DOS

Table 7.2 *Keyboard commands*

If you are using a joystick, just remember that your basic means of locomotion and interaction is through the cursor on the screen, and that you can use the joystick to move that cursor around.

For example, to move forward, maneuver the cursor to the "Forward" arrow (the one pointing up in the group of six arrows at the lower right part of the Control Panel), and then press Button A to move forward. To shoot at an object, position the cursor over it and press the joystick trigger button. To pick up or manipulate an object, move the cursor over to it and press Button A.

Well, that's about all you need to know to play this game, although solving it is quite another matter. When you find that you have reached terminal frustration, you may want to take a peak at the following solution. We have put each step of the solution in a separate paragraph. Good luck getting off that strange planet and getting back home!

Solution

The following solution assumes you are using a mouse. If not, you will have to use the arrow keys and A to activate and the Spacebar to fire.

The Roof of the Pink Building

Walk up the stairs on the side of the pink building. At the top stair, turn about 100 degrees to the left. You'll see three pyramids and a cube to your left (as shown in Figure 7.2). Shoot the pyramid nearest you. The cube will move over to the right side. Shoot the cube. Next, shoot the middle pyramid, then the last pyramid. They should all disappear, leaving a gold bar. Walk over and pick it up. Turn around and walk back down the steps.

The Colored Blocks and the Purple Walkway

Walk over to the back of the building. Six blocks of various sizes and colors will appear (see Figure 7.3). Shoot them. They will disappear to reveal a black doorway. Go through, and follow the purple walkway (carefully!) to the first moving block. Get past the four blocks without touching them (takes timing). When you reach the end, turn 90 degrees to your right. Wait for the moving green

Figure 7.2 *The pyramids on the roof*

platform to stop next to you and activate the white block on top of it. A message will appear on the bottom of the screen saying, "You are carrying some rope." (See Figure 7.4.) Turn around and go back. You cannot get onto the moving platform without falling off.

The Giant Head

Back outside, go around to the door facing the front of the building. Open it and walk inside. You will see a long hall with a moving head at the end of it and a gold bar in front of it. It will be shooting at you. Shoot its nose and it will stop. Turn around and leave. Don't try to get the gold; you will be damaged by the forcefield.

Five Gold Bars for Some Lousy Scuba Gear?

Once outside, go into the little building. There is an alien behind the counter. If activated, he will tell you he wants five gold bars for some scuba gear. Walk around to the rear of the room and crouch down. (Click the right mouse button on the "look down" arrow.) Turn to the right, and you will see a little passageway under the counter. Walk down it. You will see a gray square on the floor. Activate it and a little opening will appear. Walk into the opening, down the little hall that appears, up

Figure 7.3 *Colored blocks blocking the walkway*

Figure 7.4 *The rope platform*

the stairs, and you'll find yourself in the head's mouth. Walk out and pick up the gold brick. The forcefield is still there, so be careful. Turn to your right and you will see an orange square on the wall. Walk over and activate it. It will turn green, indicating that the forcefield is deactivated. Walk down the hallway and out the door.

More Gold

When you leave, you'll see a covered passageway coming out of the left wall. Go in, crouching if necessary. When you get inside, shoot the three pyramids on the ceiling and walk through. When you come out the other side, pick up the gold bar (for a total of three so far). (See Figure 7.5.)

Walk over to the signpost and activate it. It may take a couple of attempts from different directions, but eventually you'll tie your rope on and slide down into a waiting dinghy. Activate the motor. When you start moving, turn to your left. You will see a gold bar in some rocks on your left. Try to grab it as you go past. Don't worry if you miss; just activate the motor when you get to the lighthouse again and you'll come back. You can go back and forth between the lighthouse and the cliff until you have it. Once you have the gold bar and you reach the lighthouse, turn around on the boat and walk into the water. Wait a few seconds, and everything will turn black.

The Desert Island

Next thing you know, you're on a desert island with a chest, a palm tree, and a gold bar. Take the gold. Walk over under the palm tree and shoot the coconut. It will fall and break open, revealing a wooden key. Take both, the key and coconut. The wooden key is of no value, but you get points for it. Walk over to the other side of the palm tree and walk into it. You'll climb it, and when you reach the top you'll see a gold key. Get it and climb back down. Walk over and activate the chest, which will open. Climb in it, and you'll appear back at the lighthouse. Get back in the dinghy and go back to the cliffs. You can climb back up by just stepping into the water next to the rope.

The Expensive Scuba Gear

Now go back to the store and buy the scuba gear with your five gold bars. Go back to the cliff and activate the signpost again. Climb back down into the dinghy. Activate it and go back to the light-house. Walk around to the back of the lighthouse and open the door. Walk inside and you'll change into the scuba gear. Leave the room and walk into the water.

Figure 7.5 *The third gold bar*

Ticket to Ride

You'll see a shark and a fish swimming towards you. Wait till they get near you and activate the fish. This may take a couple of tries. The fish will hand (or "fin") you an exit pass. Go back up to the surface and you'll appear in the lighthouse. Get back in the dinghy and go back to the starting area where the store is.

Conclusion

Go through the one door you haven't gone in, the big black one. You will see a space shuttle on the other side of a small wall and a red triangle on the wall. Walk over and activate the triangle. The small wall will disappear, letting you walk out towards the shuttle. When you get near, the shuttle will take off. The End!

FOR MORE INFO

Lemme Out of Here! is a game created using DoMark's Virtual Reality Studio, a PC program that lets you create complicated virtual worlds. You can reach DoMark directly at:

DoMark Software Limited
Ferry House
51-57 Lacy Road,
Putney, London, SW15 1PR
Int Tel: 44 81 7872222

Virtual Reality Studio is distributed in North America by Accolade. For more information, contact:

Caryn Mical
Accolade, Inc.
550 South Winchester Blvd.
San Jose, CA 95128
(408) 246-6607

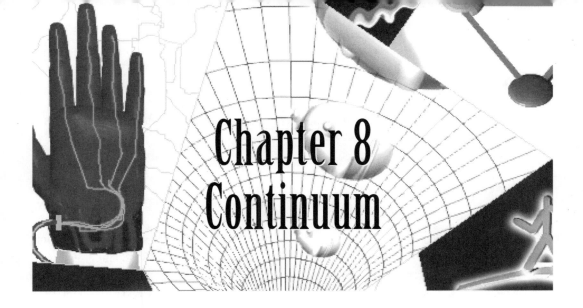

Chapter 8
Continuum

You can have a lot of fun with this one. Continuum is a game that takes place in a three-dimensional world. The object of the game is to maneuver your character (called a "mobile") around the 3-D environment, going from room to room and collecting prize crystals and other goodies as you do so.

This demo version of Continuum does not include all the rooms or features of the commercial version, but it will give you a sampling of the flavor of the game. For example, you can choose to control one of six mobiles, or select from a total of six different display variables, including viewing the entire proceedings from the mobile's point of view. We cover these options in greater detail below.

UP AND RUNNING

To use the Continuum demo, make sure you are in the proper directory (or the disk containing the file is in the current drive), and type:

Continu (Enter)

In a few moments, you will see the following menu:

Select Video Card

F1	CGA	4 Colors
F2	EGA	16 Colors
F3	Tandy	16 Colors
F4	Hercules	2 Colors
F5	VGA	16 Colors

Press a Function Key

To continue, press the function key corresponding to the video card you are using. This results in the following Main Menu:

```
F1        Game
F2        Select Video Card
F3        Return to DOS

Press a Function Key
```

You've just specified your video card, and you've just escaped from DOS, so the only reasonable alternative at this point is F1: Game. This takes you into the demo version of Continuum.

To play Continuum, press Enter when the highlight bar is over GAME. The next screen lets you choose between ACTION, EMOTION, TOP SCORES, and LOAD GAME. Choose ACTION or EMOTION to play the game (you can read more about these options below).

OF SOUND BOARDS AND SYSTEM BEEPS

Although a sound board is not a requirement for this game, it is highly recommended. The difference in sound and music quality between the built-in IBM speaker and a sound board is like the difference between a kazoo and a symphony orchestra. If you are not using a sound board on your PC, the first thing you will want to do is turn off the relentless beeps that accompany the game.

To turn off the music, you first have to get into the game (by selecting ACTION or EMOTION), and then press Esc to go to the Options Menu. Use the arrow keys to move the highlight bar to Options, and press Enter. Now move the highlight bar to Music On and press Enter to change it to Music Off. Press Esc to go back to the previous screen, and Esc again to get back to the game. If you don't have a sound board, you will thank us for putting this information up front. More about the Options Menu below.

USING THE SOFTWARE

As we mentioned earlier, you are controlling one of six mobiles as you navigate around a 3-D world, picking up crystals and going from room to room. You start off with three minutes on the clock. Each time you enter a new room, you are given an extra sixty seconds. You are also rewarded with an extra sixty seconds each time you score 10,000 points. You score points for "Flight Time," or time your mobile is airborne. The longer your mobile is in flight, the more points you receive. You also score points for collecting the crystals and cubes scattered throughout the 3-D environment. Capturing a crystal gives you 10,000 points right off the bat. See Figure 8.1 for the main game screen.

Because you are in a 3-D environment, your mobile can bounce up and down as well as move around on the floor of each room. The mobile bounces only when it is on one of the many colored

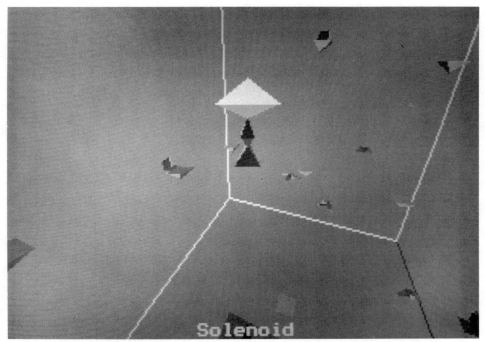

Figure 8.1 *Maneuver your mobile around by bouncing it from platform to platform. Gain extra points for keeping your mobile airborne*

platforms scattered at various levels around the room. As you bounce, momentum causes your mobile to bounce higher and higher, as you were on a trampoline. If you should fall off your platform, you will fall to the floor of the room with a resounding *thud*. You won't die, but you'll stop bouncing, and you will need to maneuver your mobile to one of the platforms on the floor. From there you need to start bouncing all over again, jumping on to the higher platforms until you reach the exit door.

Once you achieve some elevation, you can use the controls to guide your mobile like a glider from platform to platform. Remember that one way to score points is to keep your mobile airborne as long as possible (but without falling back onto the floor).

CONTROLLING YOUR MOBILE

You can control your mobile using either a joystick or the keyboard. Table 8.1 is a summary of the relevant commands:

ACTION	KEYBOARD	JOYSTICK
Forward Thrust	**Spacebar**	**Fire Button**
Left Turn	**Left Arrow**	**Left**
Right Turn	**Right Arrow**	**Right**
Rotate Camera Up	**Up Arrow**	**Up**
Rotate Camera Down	**Down Arrow**	**Down**

Table 8.1 Keyboard and joystick commands

Rotating the camera allows you to scan the room you are in without affecting your mobile's movement.

ACTION VERSUS EMOTION

In the commercial version of Continuum you can choose to play in ACTION mode or in EMOTION mode. ACTION mode is a full-blown arcade game, with the clock ticking and points mounting. EMOTION mode, on the other hand, is for those who just want to explore the Continuum universe without the pressure of clocks or points.

Although EMOTION mode is one of the options in the demo version of Continuum, it does not give you unlimited exploration of the Continuum universe. Only one area (the "Dream" area) is available for exploration, and even that is not available for an unlimited time. We therefore suggest you play Continuum in ACTION mode. If you feel an overpowering need to explore all 256 rooms of the Continuum universe, you might consider buying the commercial version. Meanwhile, you can still have a lot of fun playing with the demo version.

GAME OPTIONS

Game Options gives you control over a number of gameplay features. To access the Game Options Menu, press Esc at any time during the game. This brings up the following menu:

```
MEMORY RECALL
MEMORIZE
SAVE GAME
OPTIONS
MAP
MAIN MENU
```

To select an option, use the Up and Down Arrow keys to highlight it, and then press Enter to make your selection.

Memory Recall: Restores the game to the exact state it was in when it was last Memorized (see next item). This allows you to try a difficult maneuver or enter a dangerous area without fear of being forced back to Square One.

Memorize: This lets you experiment with different strategies without risking the entire game. If your strategy should fail, select Memory Recall (see previous item) to take you back to the exact same state. Note that Memorize and Memory Recall are temporary, and remain in effect only while the current game is active. To save a game to disk, see Save Game, below.

Save Game: You can save a game in progress by selecting this option. You will be prompted to provide a name for your saved game. Continuum will then save the game into the current directory. To load a saved game, go to the Main Menu (see below) and select Load Game.

Options: Choosing Options brings up a submenu of additional choices. This submenu lets you choose from six different mobiles, lets you turn the sound or music on or off, and gives you some additional display options. To select an item from this submenu, use the Up and Down Arrow keys to highlight the item, and then press Enter. This will either toggle between two states (as in the Sound and Music options) or produce further options. When you have finished making your adjustments, press Esc to back up one menu at a time until you return to the game.

- Sound: Pressing Enter toggles between Sound On and Sound Off. Press Esc when the desired state is showing.

- Music: Pressing Enter toggles between Music On and Music Off. Press Esc when the desired state is showing. As we mentioned earlier, Continuum is best played with a sound board. If you don't have one, you may want to turn the music off in a hurry.

- Mobile: Pressing Enter brings up a selection screen giving you six choices for a mobile, with the current one highlighted. Use the Left and Right Arrow keys to highlight the desired mobile, and then press Enter to use that selection.

- Display Options: Lets you choose from a variety of display options. Pressing Enter brings up the submenu shown below. Highlight the items you wish to modify by using the Up and Down Arrow keys, and then press Enter to toggle between the two display options. When you have made all the desired adjustments, press Esc to accept them and return to the previous menu.

- Filled/Vector Background: Choosing Filled displays the floors, walls, and ceilings in solid colors. Choosing Vector displays the same background elements in outline form. Choose the background style that works best with your system.

- Filled/Wire Forms: Similar to the background display options, you can choose to display your mobile as well as the platforms, cubes, and crystals as filled or wireframe objects.

- Lock/Unlock Mobile: This is not really a display option, since it affects the way the mobile behaves under your control. If the mobile is Locked, it stops rotating as soon as you release the Left or Right Arrow key. If the mobile is Unlocked, it continues to spin freely for a short while even after you release the control keys.

- Lock/Unlock Camera: You can rotate the camera up or down by pressing the Up and Down Arrow keys. This allows you to scan the room without affecting the behavior of the mobile. With the camera Locked, it will always return to its default or neutral position when you move to the next room. To maintain manual control over the camera, choose Unlocked. In that mode, the camera will remain in the position you specify until you change it again (or until you select Locked).

- Camera Vertical/Slant-On: When the camera is set to Vertical, your view is always parallel to the ground, regardless of your direction. With the camera set to Slant-On, it will swerve and bank with your mobile as you make left or right turns.

- Observer/Mobile View: You can choose between Observer View, which is a third person perspective showing your mobile as well as the other elements in the room, and Mobile View, which shows the world through the eyes of the mobile.

You can add a greater degree of difficulty to the game by choosing from the above display options. For a particularly challenging game, you may want to try your hand using the following settings:

- Vector Background

- Wire Forms

- Unlock Mobile

- Unlock Camera

- Camera Slant-On

- Mobile View

- Map: This option is available only in ACTION mode. By selecting Map, you can view a top-down map of the Continuum universe. A colored circle shows the room you currently occupy, while all the rooms you have visited are shown blacked out. The number of cubes and crystals remaining are shown on either side of the map.

FOR MORE INFO

Continuum is a demo version of a game by the same name published by DataEast, computer game publisher and video game manufacturer. You can contact DataEast at:

DataEast
1850 Little Orchard Street
San Jose, CA 95125
(408) 286-7074

Chapter 9
MiG-29 Fulcrum

MiG-29 Fulcrum is the demo version of a flight simulator published by DoMark International. Because it is a demo version, it does not contain the missions and combat capability of the commercial version. It does, however, have excellent graphics and maneuverability, and lets you fly a MiG jet around at supersonic speeds.

UP AND RUNNING

To use the MiG-29 demo, make sure you are in the MIG29 directory (or the disk containing the file is on the current drive), and type:

MIG29 (Enter)

In a few moments, you will see a rendition of Red Square, as shown in Figure 9.1, followed by the main screen (see Figure 9.2)

Here you are, sitting on the runway, your jet engine emitting a throaty hum. (If you can't hear it, press N to turn the engine sound on; press N a second time to toggle it off). Before you take off, you need to decide if you are going to use the keyboard or a joystick. The program defaults to joystick, so if you have one installed on your PC, you need take no further action—just skip to the section later on Taking Off.

If you want to use the keyboard to fly your MiG jet, you will need to switch over to keyboard mode. To do that, press Control-K (press K while holding down the Control key). You can always switch back to joystick mode at any time, by pressing Control-J. You may want to do this even if you don't have a joystick installed, because joystick mode lets you use the keypad numbers (and the arrow keys) for other views from your aircraft, whereas keyboard mode reserves those keys for maneuvering the aircraft. More about this a little later.

Figure 9.1 *Red Square*

Taking Off

As soon as you are ready to take off (and you are in the correct mode), press the = key several times to increase your throttle and start your aircraft moving forward. If you like, you can press Shift-= (+) to go directly to maximum throttle. Your aircraft will start to taxi down the runway, slowly at first, and then faster and faster. When you reach a land speed of about 200 km/h (the digital readout at the upper left of the heads-up display), start pulling back on your joystick (or press the Down Arrow key) to give you an upward thrust and get you off the ground.

As soon as you have reached an altitude of a few hundred feet, you can retract your landing gear to conserve fuel and to improve your maneuverability. To do this, press L. Note that the display at the lower left of the cockpit (the plane icon) reacts accordingly, indicating that the landing gear is now retracted.

At this point, you can also turn on the autostabilizer by pressing A. With the autostabilizer turned on, you can climb and bank without having to manually level the aircraft. The light at the lower right of the cockpit glows orange to indicate that the autostabilizer is on.

From this point on, you can fly around at will, exploring the small islands and atolls in your immediate vicinity. Even though this demo version has no missions or combat, there is still plenty of chal-

Figure 9.2 *MiG-29 cockpit*

lenge in trying to fly back to base and land. The following keyboard commands are available to you as you fly your aircraft:

Views

In joystick mode, the keypad lets you see 360 degrees around your aircraft. Press 6 for the view to the right, 2 for the view behind the aircraft, and 4 for the view to the left. The 9, 3, 1, and 7 keys perform similar functions, providing views in the corresponding directions. Press 8 for the forward view with the Head-down display (the cockpit instrumentation), or 5 for the forward view without the head-down display. Tables 9.1 through 9.7 summarize the various controls.

V	View from the outside, showing the plane from the rear
M	View from the missile
J	Jump to Enemy View (not working on demo version)

Table 9.1 *Additional views*

Control-K	Select Keyboard control
Control-J	Select switched joystick control
Control-I	Select analog joystick control

Table 9.2 Joystick controls

Z	Center joystick
< >	Rudder left and right
B	Air brakes
=	Throttle up
Shift-=	Maximum Throttle
-	Throttle down
Shift -	Minimum Throttle
E	Toggle engine On/Off
L	Toggle landing gear Up/Down
W	Toggle wheel brakes On/Off
Kpad +	Pitch trim up
Kpad -	Pitch trim down
Kpad Enter	Zero pitch trim

Table 9.3 Flight controls

H	Toggle Heads-Up Display On/Off
A	Toggle Autostabilizer On/Off

Table 9.4 Instrument controls

Spacebar	Fire canon
#	Fire currently selected weapon
Backspace	Cycle current weapon:
	S-240: Two unguided rockets
	AA-8: Air to air heat-seeking missile
	AS-7: Air to surface heat-seeking missile
Enter	Select target (not working on demo version)

Table 9.5 Weapon controls

F	Drop flare
C	Drop chaff

Table 9.6 Counter measures

N	Toggle engine sound On/Off
Q	Toggle all sound On/Off
P	Pause/Resume
X	Toggle speed-up On/Off

Table 9.7 Simulation controls

FOR MORE INFO

MiG-29 Fulcrum is a flight simulator published by DoMark Software Limited. You can reach Do-Mark directly at:

DoMark Software Limited
Ferry House
51-57 Lacy Road
Putney, London, SW15 1PR
Int Tel: 44 81 7872222

MiG-29 Fulcrum is distributed in North America by Accolade. For more information, contact:

Caryn Mical
Accolade, Inc.
550 South Winchester Blvd.
San Jose, CA 95128
(408) 246-6607

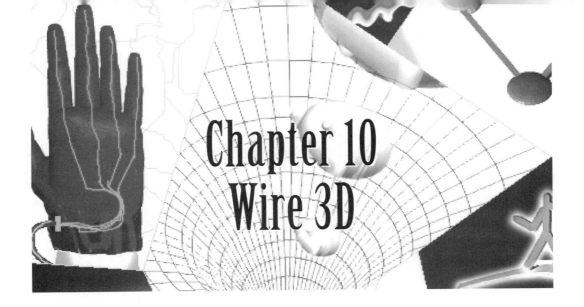

Chapter 10
Wire 3D

Wire 3D is a simple but effective application for creating 3-D images that can be viewed with red-and-blue glasses. Wire 3D uses the anaglyphic technique that we described earlier, in which each eye receives a slightly different image. By receiving a different perspective for each eye, the brain is fooled into believing that the images come from a three-dimensional object. We have included a pair of red-blue 3-D glasses specifically for viewing the Wire 3D images.

Once you have the 3-D image on the screen, you can rotate it about any of its three axes, you can shrink or expand it, or you can move it closer or farther away from you. (See table on the following page for the keyboard commands for these functions). And if you are technically inclined, Appendix C describes how to create your own 3-D images for viewing in Wire 3D.

UP AND RUNNING

To use the Wire 3D demo, first make sure you are in the WIRE3D directory (or the disk containing the file is in the current drive). If you are using a VGA monitor, you can choose to view the 3-D images either on a dark background (the default) or on a light background. In the default mode, areas where the images overlap are displayed in purple, an additive combination that looks like either blue or red through the corresponding filters. If you are not using a VGA monitor, you must use the default (dark background) mode.

To start Wire 3D with a dark background, type:

`NORMAL.BAT` (Enter)

(You can also use DARKBK.BAT, which does the same thing.)

To view the 3-D objects against a light background (VGA only), type:

`LIGHTBK.BAT` (Enter)

In this mode the background is purple and the overlapping areas are black, but the 3-D effect is otherwise identical.

In a few moments, you will see the menu shown in Table 10.1.

Select a Figure:

A Cube	B Lissa00	C Lissa01	D Lissa10	E Lissa11	F Lissa20
G Lissa21	H Lissa22	I Lissa9	J Octa	K Sphere	L Spiral
M Spiral1	N Spiral2	O Spiral3	P Spiral4	Q Spiral5	R Spiral6
S VRPlay					

Esc Exit

Table 10.1 *Menu*

To view one of the nineteen figures, just press the corresponding key.

USING THE SOFTWARE

Once the figure is displayed on the screen, you can move and rotate it using the numeric keypad. Table 10.2 summarizes the keyboard commands:

4	Rotate Left (Also Left Arrow)
6	Rotate Right (Also Right Arrow)
8	Rotate Up (Also Up Arrow)
2	Rotate Down (Also Down Arrow)
3	Rotate Clockwise
9	Rotate Counterclockwise
7	Return to Original State (Also Home)
/	Shrink Object
*	Expand Object
0	Move Object Farther Away
.	Move Object Closer
+	Speed up rate of rotation
-	Slow down rate of rotation

Table 10.2 *Keyboard commands*

Although expanding the object (*) and moving it closer (.) appear to have the same effect, they are actually quite different. Try moving the object closer and at the same time shrinking it with /. Note that moving the object closer enhances the 3-D effect. However, the closer it gets, the more difficult it becomes to merge the images.

You can further modify Wire 3D by changing the interocular distance, which defaults to 620 mm. To change this value, press Enter. Wire 3D will then prompt you to enter a new value. Increasing the interocular distance is actually equivalent to moving the object closer to the eye and at the same time shrinking it. Thus, while higher values may tend to enhance the 3-D effect, they also make it harder to converge the images to create a single object.

h, ?	**Help**
ESC, q, Q, Ctrl-C	**Main Menu (Esc again to return to DOS)**

Table 10.3 Other commands

FOR MORE INFO

Matthias Grabiak, the programmer who created Wire 3D, has generously consented to let us include the source code on our disk. This makes it easy for other programmers to incorporate some of his routines into their own code. Mr. Grabiak has also provided us with instructions for using Wire 3D to create additional 3-D objects. Readers who are technically inclined can turn to Appendix B for more information.

You can reach Mr. Grabiak via email through his CompuServe account: 74040,716.

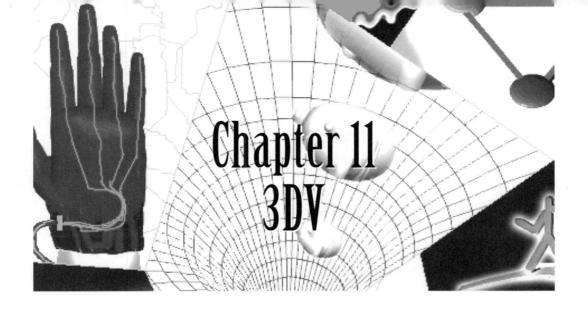

Chapter 11
3DV

3DV (or 3-D Viewer) is a simple little program that lets you manipulate 3-D objects on the screen. It does not require 3-D glasses (it does not use the anaglyphic technique), and it works with all kinds of displays, including VGA, EGA, CGA, and Hercules. It does, however, require a mouse, since all program functions, including loading datafiles as well as manipulating the objects, are carried out by pointing, clicking, and dragging.

UP AND RUNNING

To use the 3DV demo, make sure you are in the 3DV directory (or the disk containing the file is in the current drive), and type:

3DV (Enter)

In a few moments, you will see the following screen:

3-D Viewer

Version 2.5 – Copyright (c) 1988, 1991 Oscar Garcia

GRAPHICS MODE	PROJECTION
▪ EGA/VGA	▪ Perspective
▪ CGA High Resolution	▪ Orthogonal
▪ CGA Low Resolution	
▪ Hercules	

```
                          •        FILE:
      •   SHOW             •        EXIT
```

Select options by clicking mouse button

To load a file, move the cursor to the "bullet" symbol to the left of the FILE box and click the mouse button. This causes the following file menu to pop up, listing the available 3DV files:

```
2SKULLS.3-D
DATA.3DV
GALAXY.3-D
GLASS.3-D
HEIGHTS.3-D
HOUSE.3DV
SHUTTLE.3DV
SKULL.3-D
SOLIDS.3-D
SURFACE.3-D
TREE1.3DV
```

To load a file, click the filename, and then click the bullet next to SHOW. (Actually, because the program automatically moves the cursor to the SHOW bullet as soon as you click a filename, all you have to do is point to the filename and click twice.)

When the selected file has loaded, you can rotate it on the screen by dragging the mouse left and right or forward and back. You can go back to the menu screen by clicking the mouse button at any time. Select another file by following the above procedure.

You can now go ahead and explore, loading each of the various figures and making them spin around. Try looking at the figures under a Perspective projection (by clicking the Perspective bullet at the upper right part of the screen), or under an orthogonal projection.

FOR MORE INFO

3DV was created by Oscar Garcia and generously made available to interested parties for private use. For more information, you can contact Mr. Garcia directly:

Oscar Garcia
1 Clyde Street
Rotorua
New Zealand
Mr. Garcia's electronic address is garciao@mof.govt.nz.

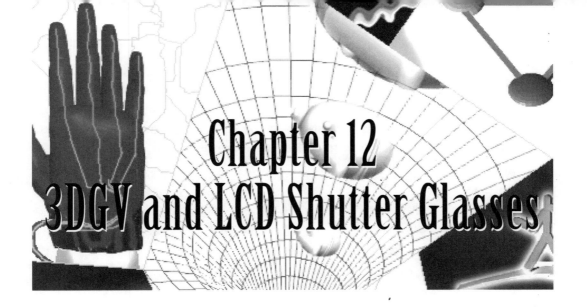

Chapter 12
3DGV and LCD Shutter Glasses

3DGV is a simple program that displays images for viewing with the modified Sega LCD shutter glasses. If you don't have a pair of these glasses, then 3DGV is probably not much use to you, unless you can alternately wink each eye sixty times per second. If you do have a modified pair of Sega glasses, 3DGV will let you load an image and then view it with the glasses. We have included instructions for modifying the Sega LCD shutter glasses following the description of the 3-GV software.

UP AND RUNNING

To use the 3DGV demo, make sure you are in the 3DGV directory (or the disk containing the file is in the current drive). Because 3DGV is still under development, you may need to work a little harder to get it going. To begin with, 3DGV does not auto-detect your video board, so you need to tell it which board you are using, and how much video RAM you have. (If you don't know what all this stuff means, and if you don't have a modified pair of Sega LCD shutter glasses connected to your parallel port, then you shouldn't even be reading this.)

The 3DGV directory contains two .GIF files. These (Left.GIF and Right.GIF) are loaded and viewed as a pair.

To view the left and right .GIF files, type the following, substituting the correct parameter values from the table that follows:

```
3DGV LEFT.GIF RIGHT.GIF -d -s (Enter)
```

The -d parameter, which specifies the display board, must be followed by two characters, the first for the board type, and the second for its resolution. Select from the following values in Table 12.1

FIRST CHARACTER	SECOND CHARACTER
1: Basic VGA	1: 320x200
3: Tseng 3000	2: 320x400
4: Tseng 4000	3: 360x480
7: Video 7	4: 640x400
9: Paradise	5: 640x480
C: Chips and Tech	6: 800x600
F: Trident	

Table 12.1 *Values*

The -s parameter specifies the video RAM. Because 3DGV displays two images in rapid succession, you need twice as much video RAM as you normally would. The -s parameter must be followed by either 5 (for 512K video RAM) or 10 (for 1024K video RAM). To specify the parallel port, you will need to add -p followed by 1 or 2 (for parallel port 1 or parallel port 2). You can also specify the parallel port address in hex. If you wish, you can add a further parameter, -i, which inverts the left and right images.

For example, if your Sega glasses are connected to parallel port 1 and you are using a Paradise video card with 1024K video RAM and a resolution of 640x480, you would type:

```
3DGV LEFT.GIF RIGHT.GIF –d95 –s10 –p1»Enter...
```

This will load the left and right images and display them for viewing with the Sega glasses.

FOR MORE INFO

3DGV was created by John Swenson, who has generously made it available for inclusion in this book. For more information, you can contact him directly through his CompuServe address:

John Swenson CompuServe 75300,2136

CONVERTING THE SEGA 3-D GLASSES ADAPTER FOR USE WITH A PARALLEL PORT

Building this circuit requires some experience with a soldering iron. If you don't have experience with this kind of tinkering, we recommend you double-check the circuit with a digital multimeter before plugging it in to your computer. For obvious reasons, we cannot accept any responsibility if the circuit you build damages your equipment. If you are in doubt, don't try it.

You will need the glasses and adapter card from Sega, a power supply (producing 5 volts and something between 10 and 12 volts [all DC]) a male DB25 connector, and some wire.

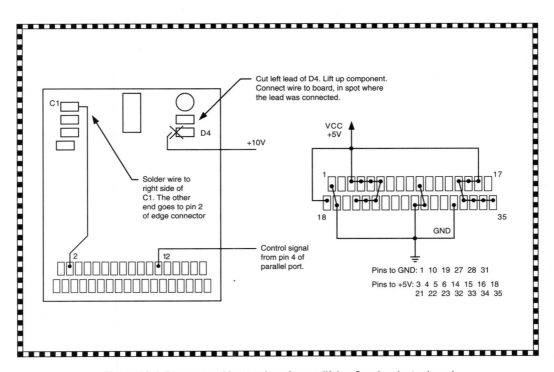

Figure 12.1 *Diagram and instructions for modifying Sega's adapter board*

The tools you will need are a soldering iron, long-nose pliers, and a wire cutter. Figure 12.1 shows a diagram of the adapter board.

The control wire gets connected to pin 4 of the DB25, and GND gets connected to pins 18 through 25. See Figure 12.2 for the pinout of the connector. Remember, the drawing is as you see it with the solder side of the pins facing you.

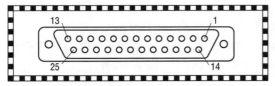

Figure 12.2 *Pinouts for DB25 connector*

The power supply: You can either get voltages you need from the PC, or use an external supply. The connectors that plug into disk drives will power this quite nicely, but you have to get the cable out of the machine somehow. If you want to use an external power supply, the 5- and 12-volt versions are fairly common; or you can make one from parts at Radio Shack. It consists of the 9-volt DC transformer (one of those big black cubes that plugs into the wall, with a wire coming out). This actually produces 9.7 volts, which is close enough to run the glasses. You will also need a 7805 3-pin regulator to produce the 5 volts (see package for details on how to hook it up).

These instructions were based on material provided by John Swenson, who welcomes your comments. Please write to him directly at:

John Swenson CompuServe 75300,2136

Appendix A
Vendors and Suppliers
of Virtual Reality Products

BATTLETECH

Battletech is a virtual reality environment where players battle against each other. Each player assumes control of a 30-foot-tall "BattleMech," an electronic alter ego which can explore up to 100 square miles of virtual terrain and battle other BattleMechs similarly controlled by other players. This is cyberspace on a grand scale.

For more information, contact:

Virtual World Entertainments
1026 W. Van Buren
Chicago, IL 60607
(312) 243-5660

CONVOLVOTRON 3D AUDIO SYSTEM

The Convolvotron is a digital audio signal processing system that reinforces the virtual environment by enabling complementary audio stimulation. The PC-compatible system uses headphones to feed sound to users.

For more information, contact:

Crystal River Engineering, Inc.
12350 Wards Ferry Road
Groveland, CA 95321
(209) 962-6382

CRYSTALEYES

CrystalEyes eye wear enables users to view computer images with three-dimensional perception. CrystalEyes provides stereoscopic imaging by using infrared signals to synchronize left and right images with liquid crystal shuttered lenses.

For more information, contact:

StereoGraphics Corporation
2171-H East Francisco Boulevard
San Rafael, CA 94901
(415) 459-4500

CYBEREDGE JOURNAL

CyberEdge Journal is a bi-monthly newsletter that focuses on technological issues and developments related to virtual reality and human-computer interaction.

For more information, contact:

CyberEdge Journal
928 Greenhill Road
Mill Valley, CA 94941
(415) 383-2458

DATAEAST

DataEast publishes the commercial version of Continuum, the 3-D bouncing game included in our software package.

For more information, contact:

DataEast
1850 Little Orchard Street
San Jose, CA 95125
(408) 286-7074

DIMENSION INTERNATIONAL

The Dimension International virtual reality system (Virtual Reality Toolkit) was used to create the Superscape demo included on our disk. Dimension International markets a number of virtual reality solutions, including Desktop virtual reality, a complete hardware/software turnkey system.

You can contact Dimension directly at:

Dimension International
Zephyr One, Calleva Park
Aldermaston, Berkshire, RG7 4QW
Int Tel: 44 734 810077; Int fax: 44 734 816940

DOMARK

DOMARK is the developer and publisher of MiG29, the flying simulation game and of Virtual Reality Studio, the world builder product that was used to create the game Lemme Out of Here!. DOMARK's products are distributed in North America by Accolade.

For more information, contact:

Caryn Mical
Accolade Inc.
550 South Winchester Blvd.
San Jose, CA 95128
(408) 246-6607

MACROMIND/PARACOMP

MacroMind/Paracomp publishes 3-D modeling, animation, and rendering software, including MacroMind Director, MacroMind Three-D, and Swivel 30.

For more information, contact:

MacroMind/Paracomp
600 Townsend, Suite 310
San Francisco, CA 94103
(415) 442-0200

FLOGISTON CHAIR

The Flogiston Chair, based on principals of posture, balance, equilibrium, and energy, enables users to focus their senses on the virtual environment.

For more information, contact:

Flogiston Corporation
462 Capehill
Webster, TX 77598
(713) 280-8554

FOCAL POINT

FOCAL POINT digital audio processing card uses audio stimulus to enhance virtual reality. Boasting a Midi3D controller, the product manages synthesizer, sampler, and disc file sounds within the 3D environment.

For more information, contact:

FOCAL POINT 3-D Audio
1402 Pine Avenue, Suite 127
Niagara Falls, NY 14301
(416) 963-9188

MANDALA

MANDALA Virtual Reality Authoring Software is a multimedia interface package that lets users interact within a virtual environment. Through audio/visual processing, the virtual environment is able to react instantly to the gestures of the user's imported video image.

For more information, contact:

The Vivid Group
317 Adelaide Street West, Suite 302
Toronto, Ontario, Canada M5V1P9
(416) 340-9290

MICRO SYNECTIC, INC.

Micro Synectic is the developer of Stare-EO, the random-dot stereogram paint program. Stare-EO is published by NE Thing.

For more information, contact:

Micro Synectic Inc.
Plaza of the Americas
Suite 318 LB 385
700 N. Pearl
Dallas, TX 75201
(214) 606-3000

NE THING ENTERPRISES

NE Thing publishes Stare-EO, the random-dot stereogram paint program. NE Thing is currently developing a line of products based on the random-dot 3-D concept, including posters and calendars.

For more information, contact:

NE Thing Enterprises
19A Crosby Drive
Bedford, MA 01730
(617) 577-1101

PHOTOVR

PhotoVR is a virtual reality package for desktop systems that loads graphic images quickly into a virtual environment, then updates the motion and orientation of the graphic image in near-real-time.

For more information, contact:

Straylight Corporation
150 Mount Bethel Road
Warren, NJ 07059
(908) 580-0086

PRESENCE: TELEOPERATORS AND VIRTUAL ENVIRONMENTS

PRESENCE is a quarterly publication devoted to teleoperators and virtual environment systems. This periodical addresses the development and design of intuitive human-machine interfaces.

For more information, contact:

PRESENCE: Teleoperators and Virtual Environments
MIT Press Journals
Research Lab of Electronics
MIT 36-709
Cambridge, MA 02139
(617) 253-2534

SENSE8

Sense8 develops the high-end virtual reality package WorldToolKit, consisting of both hardware and software.

For more information, contact:

Sense8
1001 Bridgeway, #477
Sausalito, CA 94965
(415) 331-6318

SPECTRUM HOLOBYTE

Spectrum HoloByte is the developer of the software that runs the Virtuality machines, and the publisher of numerous computer games for various platforms.

For more information, contact:

Spectrum HoloByte
2061 Challenger Drive
Alameda, CA 94501
(510) 522-3584

STEREOGRAPHICS CORP.

StereoGraphics manufactures CrystalEyes, the LCD shutter glasses that produce flicker-free 3-D images on PC computers and closed-circuit television systems.

You can reach StereoGraphics at:

StereoGraphics Corp.
2171-H East Francisco, Blvd.
San Rafael, CA 94901
(415) 459-4500
(415) 459-3020 (Fax)

TINI ALLOY COMPANY

TiNi Alloy develops shape memory metals that are used in the manufacture of tactile feedback devices.

You can reach TiNi Alloy at:

TiNi Alloy Co.
1144 65th Street, Unit A
Oakland, CA 94608
(510) 658-3172

SPACEBALL 2003

Spaceball 2003 provides an intuitive 3D interface that allows the user to manipulate virtual environments through hand movement. Spaceware, an available set of drivers, ensures the product's compatibility with numerous commercial applications.

For more information, contact:

Spaceball Technologies Incorporated
600 Suffolk Street
Lowell, MA 01854
(508) 970-0330

VPL RESEARCH, INC.

VPL Research, Inc. manufactures and markets a Macintosh-based virtual reality system known as MicroCosm. The system, which is based on a Macintosh Quadra 9000 and which includes a head-mounted display and data gloves, retails for $58,000.

For more information, contact:

Maureen Pattarelli
VPL Research Inc.
656 Bair Island Road, Third Floor
Redwood City, CA 94063
(415) 306-1150
(415) 361-1845 (Fax)

VIRTUAL REALITY DEVELOPMENT SYSTEM

Virtual Reality Development System is a complete package that enables PC users to create and interact with 3D virtual environments in real time. This system is compatible with standard PC hardware and supports specialized hardware for increased interactivity.

For more information, contact:

VREAM, Inc.
2568 N. Clark Street, #250
Chicago, IL 60614
(312) 477-0425

VIRTUALITY ARCADE MACHINES

The Virtuality arcade machines now touring the United States are manufactured in the United Kingdom by W. Industries, and distributed in the United States by Horizon Entertainment.

For more information, contact:

Bill Freund
Horizon Entertainment
P.O. Box 14020
St. Louis, MO 63178-4020
(314) 331-6000
(314) 331-6002 (Fax)

VREAM

VREAM is developing a virtual reality system designed to work with MS-DOS based machines. VREAM's software is designed to support head-mounted displays and data gloves as well as more traditional input devices.

For more information, contact:

VREAM, Inc.
2568 N. Clark Street, #250
Chicago, IL 60614
(312) 477-0425

XTENSORY, INC.

Xtensory manufactures tactile devices for use with data gloves.

For more information, contact:

Xtensory, Inc.
140 Sunridge Drive
Scotts Valley, CA 95066
(408) 439-0600

Appendix B
Wire 3D Technical Information

By Matthias Grabiak

Wire 3D is one of the programs included on the *Virtual Reality Playhouse* disk. For information on using the product itself, refer to that section of the book. The following material is technical information about the code, and includes instructions for creating your own 3-D images for viewing with the product.

The Wire 3D directory contains the files listed in Table B.1.

A. DESCRIPTION FILES

README.DOC	A short introduction to Wire 3D
COLORS.DOC	Instructions for changing color setup
FILELIST.DOC	This file
GRAPH.DOC	

B. RUN FILES

SHOW.BAT	Calls MENU.EXE
NORMAL.BAT	Calls MENU.EXE with default color setup by deleting COLORS
DARKBK.BAT	Calls MENU.EXE with dark background by copying COLORS.0 to COLORS
LIGHTBK.BAT	Calls MENU.EXE with light background by copying COLORS.1 to COLORS
MENU.EXE	Displays a menu of figures
WIRE3-D.EXE	Main program, call as WIRE3-D figurefile

C. FIGURE FILES

VRPLAY.FIG	Miscellaneous figures
CUBE.FIG	
SPHERE.FIG	

OCTA.FIG
LISSA00.FIG
LISSA01.FIG
LISSA10.FIG
LISSA11.FIG
LISSA20.FIG
LISSA21.FIG
LISSA22.FIG
LISSA9.FIG
SPIRAL.FIG
SPIRAL1.FIG
SPIRAL2.FIG
SPIRAL3.FIG
SPIRAL4.FIG
SPIRAL5.FIG
SPIRAL6.FIG

COLORS.0	When copied to COLORS, Wire 3D displays a light figure on a dark background
COLORS.1	When copied to COLORS, Wire 3D displays a dark figure on a light background

D. SOURCE FILES

WIRE3-D.PRJ	Project file for Borland C++/Turbo C++] for creating WIRE3-D.EXE
WIRE3-D.H	Header file
WIRE3-D.CPP	Main module (completely portable)
GRAPH.CPP	Graphics module
GETCMD.CPP	Module for reading keyboard input
EGAVGA.OBJ	BGI driver
MENU.C	Source file for MENU.EXE

E. FIGURE CREATION FILES

SPHERE.EXE	Pascal program to create a sphere
SPHERE.PAS	Source for SPHERE.EXE

LISSA.EXE	Pascal program to create 3-D Lissajous figures, defined as: $x = R*\sin(n1*s+of1)$ $y = R*\sin(n2*s+of2)$ $z = R*\sin(n3*S+of3)$
LISSA.PAS	Source for LISSA.EXE
LISSA00.PRM	Miscellaneous parameter files for LISSA.EXE, to be used as LISSA <
LISSAxx.PRM	
LISSA01.PRM	
LISSA10.PRM	
LISSA11.PRM	
LISSA20.PRM	
LISSA21.PRM	
LISSA22.PRM	
LISSA9.PRM	
SPIRAL.EXE	C program to create spirals
SPIRAL.C	Source for SPIRAL.EXE
SPIRAL.PRM	Parameter file for SPIRAL.EXE, to be used as SPIRAL < SPIRALx.PRM
SPIRAL1.PRM	
SPIRAL2.PRM	
SPIRAL3.PRM	
SPIRAL4.PRM	
SPIRAL5.PRM	
SPIRAL6.PRM	

Table B.1 *Wire 3-D directory files*

OVERVIEW

WIRE3-D.EXE takes one parameter—the name of the figure description file that describes the object to be displayed. The file format is described below.

The Wire 3D directory includes the program MENU.EXE. This looks for files with the extension .FIG and lets you load one by typing the corresponding letter. The escape key (ESC) is used in both MENU.EXE and WIRE3-D.EXE. If you started WIRE3-D from within MENU, Esc returns you to the menu program.

CREATING A 3-D OBJECT

To create a figure file that describes an object, simply enter the three-dimensional coordinates that define the object. Coordinates correspond roughly to one-tenth of a millimeter. A data file of this sort can be created with any editor or with a word processor if you save it in ASCII format. The Wire 3D directory also includes several programs that create figures automatically in accordance with your parameters. These programs are described in greater detail below.

The first parameter is an integer specifying the distance of the object from the eye, or more accurately, the distance between the eye and the origin of the coordinate system. You can change this value with . or 0 while the program is running.

The next parameter is a floating point number that resizes the object. All coordinates of the object are multiplied by that number. Thus, a factor of 2 doubles the object's apparent size, while 0.5 halves it. This is particularly useful when you have entered a figure manually and you want to adjust its size. You can adjust this stretch factor by pressing / and * while the program is running.

The third parameter is the number of points or displacements that define the object. Each of these consists of three integer numbers and one letter, separated by spaces. The coordinate values x, y, and z stand for right, forward, and up for positive values, and left, backward, and down for negative values. The letter corresponds to a command.

M or m moves to a point without drawing a line, while L or l draws a line from the current point to the point specified by the coordinates. Upper case letters indicate an absolute value, that the point is directly specified by the coordinates. For example, 0 0 100 M means move to the point 10 mm above the origin, without drawing a line.

Lower case letters indicate a relative value, measured as a displacement from the previous point. For example, -200 0 0 l means draw a line moving 20 mm to the left.

An example of a complete data file that draws the three coordinate axes is shown in the table below.

The first line places the figure about 1,000 mm in front of the eyes. The second line indicates that the figure is actually bigger than the coordinates specify, by a factor of 1.5. Thus, the point 500 0 0 actually corresponds to 750 0 0.

The third line indicates that the object is described by 6 points. In the next line we move 500 units to the left of the origin. From there we draw a line to the point 50 units to the right. This displays the x-axis.

Similarly, the next two lines draw the y-axis going in the forward direction. In the second to last line we move to the point 500 units below the origin, and from there we move up by 1000 units, as in-

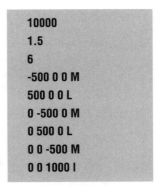

```
10000
1.5
6
-500 0 0 M
500 0 0 L
0 -500 0 M
0 500 0 L
0 0 -500 M
0 0 1000 l
```

Table B.2 Data file
for displaying coordinate axes

dicted by the last line. This has the same effect as 0 0 500 L.

Using the coordinates of the object, the program creates two images from different perspectives, using a value 620 mm for the interocular distance. To construct the two images, it uses an imaginary plane 500 mm in front of the eyes, on which the two-dimensional images are projected. Every point of the object is connected to each eye by a line, and the intersection of this line with the imaginary plane provides the corresponding point in the two-dimensional image that is displayed on the screen.

This is illustrated in Figure B.1. The corresponding data file is given in Table B.3. The imaginary plane is indicated by the rectangle. Behind that plane there is a line, shown as a double line, connected to each eye in front of the plane. This creates two triangles, with the points in front of the plane corresponding to the position of the eyes. Wherever these triangles intersect with the imaginary plane they create two lines in that plane. The left one would then be displayed in red and the right one in blue. This procedure automatically creates the right perspective views with objects farther away appearing smaller.

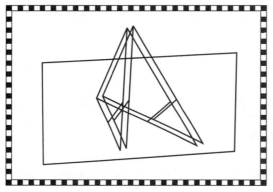

Figure B.1 *Wire 3D creates the two images by constructing an imaginary plane 500 mm in front of viewer's eyes*

| 10000 |
| 3 |
| 18 |
| 500 0 -250 M |
| 500 0 250 L |
| -500 0 250 L |
| -500 0 -250 L |
| 500 0 -250 L |
| -105 300 -100 M |
| 95 500 100 L |
| -95 300 -100 M |
| 105 500 100 L |
| 100 500 100 M |
| -140 -300 0 L |
| -100 300 -100 L |
| 140 -300 0 L |
| 100 500 100 L |
| -120 0 -50 M |
| -50 0 38 L |
| 20 0 -50 M |
| 125 0 38 L |

Table B.3 *Data file for Figure B.1*

PROGRAM DOCUMENTATION

In this section we describe the way the program works in greater detail. The program WIRE3-D.EXE is written in C++, the object-oriented extension of C.

Wire 3D contains three different modules, WIRE3D.CPP, GRAPH.CPP, and GETCMD.CPP. The main module WIRE3D.CPP is written so that it is independent of the hardware or the operating system. Thus, to rewrite the program for a different system, you just need to rewrite the module GRAPH.CPP, which is responsible for all graphics output, and GETCMD.CPP, which is responsible for the keyboard input.

Wire 3D declares a data class *figure*, which contains a linked list of another structure called *node*, corresponding to the end points of the lines. The data members of *node* are *float p[3]*, which are the coordinates or displacements; *char code*, which can be *M*, *m*, *L*, or *l*, and *node *pNext*, which is a pointer to the next node (or NULL if there are no more nodes).

The constructor *node (istream& is)* creates another node by reading the coordinates and the code from the input file *is*. The member function *NextNode* executes the command specified by the code, that is it moves the current point and possibly draws a line. The two parameters of *NextNode*, *disp* and *c*, indicate whether the image to be drawn is for the left eye or the right eye. Here *disp* is the negative displacement of the eye relative to the *x*-axis, which is *+a* for the left eye and *-a* for the right eye, with the global variable *a* being half the distance between the eyes. Here *c* specifies the color used to draw the image and is one of the constants *LeftColor* or *RightColor* defined in WIRE3-D.H. *NextNode* calls the member function *Convert2D*, which actually calculates the two-dimensional coordinates of the image in the imaginary plane. These coordinates are passed to the function *GPoint*, which displays that point on the screen. *GPoint* is defined in GRAPH.CPP. Finally *NextNode* returns the pointer to the next node. The member function *Draw* of the structure *figure* loops through all nodes by calling *NextNode*.

The member function *Convert2D* of the class *node* is the heart of the whole program, calculating the two-dimensional image from the three-dimensional coordinates of a given point of the object. First the coordinates or displacements are multiplied by the global variable *stretch*, which is initialized by the second parameter in the figure file and can be changed by the key commands / and *. The resulting vector is either stored in the static variable *v* if the code is *M* or *L*, or added to *v* in case of a displacement, i.e. for *m* or *l*. *v* is declared as static so that its value is saved for the next function call which might be a displacement.

Next the vector *v* is multiplied by the matrix *CTM* (which stands for Current Transformation Matrix), and the result is stored in the vector *v1*. The multiplication with *CTM* results in a rotation of the object. Turning the object does not actually turn the object itself, but changes the matrix *CTM*. The two-dimensional coordinates of the corresponding point in the image are calculated in the last two lines and stored in the vector *p2*. The x value is given by $l0*(v1[0]+disp)/(v1[1]+l)$ (assume that *adj* = 0 for now). The global variable *l* contains the distance to the point from the eye, so that *v1[1]+l* is the distance from the eye in the y direction. *v1[0]+disp* specifies the position of the object in the x direction relative to the current eye.

Multiplying this value by the factor $l0/(v1[1]+l)$, where l0 is the distance between the eyes and the imaginary plane, gives the x-coordinate of the intersection of the imaginary plane and the line connecting the eye with the point of the object (see Figure A.5, above). The y-coordinate is calculated in a similar way. The negative sign takes into account that for many systems, the direction of the y-coordinate is reversed, that is, it grows if you go down. One problem with the above algorithm is that the two images can be somewhat far apart, which can make it difficult to merge both images. Therefore, the two images are moved closer to each other by an amount that depends on the floating point variable *adj*. *adj=0* means that no adjustment is made whereas for *adj=1* the images are displayed on top of each other. The value of *adj* can be adjusted while running the program by pressing the J key, which prompts for a new value.

The module GRAPH.CPP defines six functions: *GInit*, *GEnd*, *GDelete*, *GShowLeft*, *GShowRight*, and *GPoint*. *GInit* and *GEnd* initialize and exit the graphics module. *GInit* tries to switch to VGA high resolution graphics and if this fails to EGA high resolution. Then it calculates the coordinates of the center of the screen as well as the aspect ratio. These values are later used by the function *GPoint*. Finally it sets the write mode to *COPY_PUT* which overwrites the screen with the current color (which is set to *MAGENTA*).

This may require some explanation. Before drawing a line on the screen, the function *GPoint* writes the value of the current color, either red or blue, to the map mask register of the video hardware with *outportb(0x3c4,2); outportb(0x3c5,color)*. In VGA or EGA mode the image on the screen is actually stored in color maps, i.e., as independent images for the red, green, and blue components. Writing a color value of red or blue to the map mask register has the effect that only that color map is accessible in the subsequent call to *lineto*. Thus, drawing the line in magenta actually has the effect of drawing it either in red or blue, with the other color component being disabled. The two following *outportb* commands reenable all other color maps.

For VGA screens, *GInit* now looks to see whether either a file named COLORS is present in the current directory or a color file is defined by the DOS environment variable WIRECOLORS. If that is the case, *GInit* opens that file and uses the values stored in it to change the color palette. That file contains four color triplets with values between 0 and 63 for the red, green, and blue content of the background color, the image for the right eye, the left eye, the overlap between the two images and the text color. These color values are assigned to the color registers that normally correspond to black, red, blue, magenta, and light gray. In that way you can change the default colors.

GPoint calculates the corresponding screen coordinates, centering the image and taking the aspect ratio into account. Then it updates the current point, and for code *L* or *l* it draws a line. *GShowRight* and *GShowLeft* are called by the member function *Show* or *figure* after the complete image for each eye is drawn. Since *GPoint* already does all the work there is nothing left to be done, so that *GShowLeft* and *GShowRight* are actually only dummy functions. They have been included in case it is necessary to do additional work on different video systems.

Back to the main module WIRE3-D. Among its data members there are L, *Stretch*, and *count,* which correspond to the first three lines in a figure description file. L is the original distance of the object from the eye and *Stretch* is the original magnification factor. These values can be restored by pressing 7, together with the original viewing angle. Here *count* is the number of defining points, and *pFirst* points to a linked list of them. The constructor creates *figure* by reading the data from a figure description file. The member function *Draw* draws one image for one eye, looping through the linked list of nodes. Finally, *Show* puts it all together by first deleting the previous screen, drawing the image for the left eye, calling *GShowLeft*, drawing the image for the right eye, and calling *GShowRight*.

The function *main,* which is called upon program entry, first checks whether a filename has been specified as a parameter. Otherwise, it displays a help screen and exits. If the specified figure file could be opened successfully, a data structure *figure* with name *Fig* is created and the data are read from the file. The next step is to initialize the current transformation matrix *CTM* to a unit matrix by calling *InitCTM*. Then the figure is displayed on the screen and the program enters a loop which gets a one-letter command from the keyboard and executes it, until it encounters Ctrl-c, q, or Esc, which ends the program.

Appendix C
Power Glove Interface for Parallel Port on IBM

The following instructions allow you to connect a Nintendo Power Glove to your PC's parallel port.

IMPORTANT: We have assembled this cable successfully following these directions. However, we cannot be responsible for any damage resulting from the use of this product in this way. Consequently, assembly of this cable and its subsequent use with the Power Glove is your sole responsibility.

THE CONNECTOR

```
      * 1
  7 * * 2
  6 * * 3     Looking AT the connector on glove cable
  5 * * 4
```

PINOUT

1: Ground
2: Clock
3: Latch
4: Data
5: N/C (lightgun)
6: N/C (lightgun)
7: +5V

CONNECTING IT TO THE PARALLEL PORT

Glove	Printer Port
1	18 GND
2	2 D0
3	3 D1
4	13 SLCT (input)

POWER

Connect pin 7 on the glove to any location with +5V from the computer. Pin 1 on any gameport is a good place. You can also use the keyboard connector. On an XT pinout, the +5V connector is pin 5, as follows:

Looking at the back of the computer:

```
3  1
5  4
   2
```

We strongly suggest you check the voltage if you are using any other configuration.

THE CABLE

We recommend buying one of the extender cables to chop up for the connector (the Curtis Super Extendo cable is around $7 for 2 cables). This makes it easy to also use other Nintendo devices and also allows testing the glove (plus you get a long cable to the control box).

CODING

We're including the latest code developed for the glove. The code is from the glove-list-mailing, an information exchange set up on internet to help solve problems with interfacing the glove. The code is commented and uses a glitch-reduction method for *very* clean sampling. You will need to adjust the N & D defines to match the timing on your machine until you get a steady sample.

The code is currently set for LPT2. (INPORT = 0x279, OUTPORT = 0x278). For LPT1, change INPORT to 0x379 and OUTPORT to 0x378.

The code is for Turbo C/C++/Borland C++. It uses the BGI library for the graphics cursor. It can be readily to Microsoft C (or other). We have put a copy of the code on the disk (in ASCII format). See *Theglove.C* on the disk.

```c
#include <dos.h>
#include <bios.h>
#include <stdio.h>
#include <conio.h>
#include <graphics.h>

int gdriver = VGA;              /* for graphics plot and cursor */
int gmode = VGAHI;

#define XHYST 2                 /* hysterisis for X, Y low noise reduction */
#define YHYST 2                 /* 2 eliminates +/-3 quanta of noise */

#define XACC 8                  /* X, Y maximum accel/decel level. Should */
#define YACC 8                  /* be 6-10, but too high limits gesturing */

#define XXTEND 2                /* stretches deglitching time */
#define YXTEND 1

#define N 1                     /* delay scaled by N/D <CHANGED> */
#define D 1                     /* these are 1,1 for 486 PC with i/o card */
#define INPORT  0x279           /* i/o port addresses <CHANGED> */
#define OUTPORT 0x278

/* bits for i/o ports <CHANGED> */

#define         GDATA           0x10        /* PG data in */
#define         GLATCH          0x02        /* PG latch out */
#define         GCLOCK          0x01        /* PG clock out */
#define         GCLOLAT         0x03        /* clock + latch */

/* delay values for sending and sampling data <CHANGED> */

#define    D2BYTES    150    /* delay between 2 bytes = 96 us  */
#define    D2BITS     6    /* delay between 2 bits = 3 us    */
#define    D2SLOW     8000    /* intertest delay = 2000-4000 us */

/* Delay timing: may not work in some IBM C's due to problems with LONGs */

void fdelay(unsigned int val)
{
 long i;

 i=(long)(N*val);
 for(;i>0;i-=D);
}
```

```
/* defines for output line pair control */

#define    COLO()        outportb(OUTPORT, 0)        /* clock 0 latch 0 */
#define    COL1()        outportb(OUTPORT, GLATCH)    /* clock 0 latch 1 */
#define    C1LO()        outportb(OUTPORT, GCLOCK)    /* clock 1 latch 0 */
#define    C1L1()        outportb(OUTPORT, GCLOLAT)   /* clock 1 latch 1 */


/* prototypes */

void Hires (void);                    /* puts glove in hires mode   */
void getglove (unsigned char *);      /* get data packet from glove */
int  glove_ready();                   /* returns 0 if not ready     */
                                      /* delay repeats by 2-4 ms    */
unsigned char getbyte (void);          /* read byte from glove */

/***** GLOVE DATA SPECIFICATIONS **************

The glove_data array has been simplified. These are its functions:

x =   X position, 3mm per number
y =   Y position, 3mm per number
z =   distance,  14mm per number
rot = wrist twist. 0 is up 1 is slightly CW, 5 is down, 11 is slightly CCW.
     About 30 to 40 degrees per count.

Note: exact scaling of all above change with distance! Closer is higher res.

fingers = packed 2-bit values, 0 is open, 3 is (tight) fist:
        Bit format: TtIiMmRr  for Thumb, Index, Middle, and Ring fingers.

keys: $FF or $80 is no key. Responds with 0 to 9 for keys "0" thru "9"
   $82 = START, $83 = SEL, $0A = "A", $0B = "B", 0 is "Center"
   Up,down,left,right are $0D,$0E,$0C,$0F respectively.

*/

typedef struct glove_data {
                    signed char x,y,z,rot,fingers,keys;
                    } glove_data;

/*******************************************/

void main ()
{
 unsigned char buf[12];
 glove_data   *glov;
 unsigned unready;                    /* number of unsuccessful tries to read glove */
```

```
  glov=(glove_data *)buf;
  initgraph(&gdriver, &gmode, "d:\\tpas5\\bgidrvs\\"); /* VGA graphics, 640x480 */
  cleardevice();
                                    /* begin again here if glove crashes */
  restart:
  Hires ();                                /* set PG into 'hires' mode */

  while(!kbhit())
   {
    unready = 0;                            /* start polling glove */
    fdelay(D2SLOW);
    while(glove_ready()==0)                 /* wait for glove to become ready */
     {
      if (unready++>500) goto restart;       /* reset mode if dead glove */
      fdelay(D2SLOW);              }

    getglove(buf);                          /* read 6 byte packet */
    gotoxy(1,1);                            /* print xyz at scrren top */
    printf("% 4d % 4d % 4d   ", 255&glov->x, 255&glov->y, 255&glov->z);
                                  /* print rot, fingers, keys */
    printf("%-2x %-2x %-2x ", buf[3],buf[4],buf[5]);

    deglitch(glov);               /* remove spikes and jumps */
    dehyst(glov);                 /* add hysteresis to remove LL noise */

    drawp(glov);                  /* plot x,y positions */
    drawthing(glov);              /* animate glove cursor */
   }

  getch();                        /* exit when keyboard hit */
  COLO();                         /* release glove on exit */
}


void getglove(buf)        /* read 6 byte data packet */
unsigned char *buf;
{
 register unsigned char *bp;

 bp = buf;

 *bp++ = getbyte ();       /* read data */
 fdelay(D2BYTES);
 *bp++ = getbyte ();
 fdelay(D2BYTES);
 *bp++ = getbyte ();
 fdelay(D2BYTES);
 *bp++ = getbyte ();
 fdelay(D2BYTES);
 *bp++ = getbyte ();
```

```
 fdelay(D2BYTES);
 *bp++ = getbyte ();
 fdelay(D2BYTES);
                          /* throwaways (speeds up polling later) */
 getbyte ();
 fdelay(D2BYTES);
 getbyte ();
}


int glove_ready()        /* returns 1 if glove ready, 0 otherwise */
{
 int f;
 f = getbyte();
 return( (f==0xA0) ? 1 : 0);
}


unsigned char getbyte ()        /* read a byte from glove <rolled code> */
{
 register int i;
 register unsigned char x = 0;

 C1L0 ();                 /* generate a reset (latch) pulse */
 C1L1 ();
 fdelay(D2BITS);         /* hold for 5 us */
 C1L0 ();

 for(i=0;i<8;i++)
  {
   x=x<<1;
   x+=((inportb(INPORT)&GDATA)>>4);
   C0L0 ();
   C1L0 ();  /* pulse */
  }

 return(x);  /* return the byte */
}


/*  HIRES ENTRY CODES
byte:
1- any value between $05 and $31
2- only $C1 and $81 work OK
3- no effect
4- no effect
5- no effect
6- only $FF works
```

```
7- seems to affect read rate slightly, 1 fastest
*/

int hires_code[7] = { 0x06, 0xC1, 0x08, 0x00, 0x02, 0xFF, 0x01 };


void Hires ()   /* enter HIRES mode <rolled code- speed unimportant> */
{
 int i,j,k;
                             /* dummy read 4 bits from glove:  */
 C1L0 (); C1L1 ();           /* generate a reset (latch) pulse */
 fdelay(D2BITS);
 C1L0 ();

 fdelay(D2BITS);
 COL0 (); C1L0 ();       /* pulse clock */
 fdelay(D2BITS);
 COL0 (); C1L0 ();       /* pulse clock */
 fdelay(D2BITS);
 COL0 (); C1L0 ();       /* pulse clock */
 fdelay(D2BITS);
 COL0 (); C1L0 ();       /* pulse clock */

                         /* handshake for command code? */
 C1L0 ();
 fdelay(16950);          /* 7212 us delay */
 C1L1 ();
 fdelay(4750);           /* 2260 us delay */

 for(i=0;i<7;i++)        /* send 7 bytes */
  {
   k=hires_code[i];
   for(j=0;j<8;j++)        /* 8 bits per byte, MSB first */
    {
     if(k & 0x80)
      {
       C1L1();
       COL1();
       C1L1();
      }
     else
      {
       C1L0();
       COL0();
       C1L0();
      }
     k=k<<1;
     fdelay(D2BITS);
    }
   fdelay(D2BYTES);
```

```
 }

 fdelay(1090);              /* 892 us delay (end of 7. byte) */

 C1L0 ();                   /* drop the reset line */
 fdelay(30000);             /* some time for the glove controller to relax */
 fdelay(30000);
 }


 glove_data oldbuf;         /* used to store old state for drawing */

 int drawn = 0;             /* set if cursor to be erased */


 drawthing(glove_data *g) /* draw square cursor */
 {
  if(g->keys==2) return;   /* hold down "2" to stop drawing */

  if(drawn)                 /* erase old box */
   {
    setcolor(0);
    drawit(&oldbuf);
   }

  setcolor(15);             /* draw new box */
  drawit(g);
  drawn = 1;

  oldbuf.x = g->x;          /* save pos'n for next erase */
  oldbuf.y = g->y;
  oldbuf.z = g->z;
 }


 drawit(glove_data *g)   /* draw/erase box cursor */
 {
  int x = 320+2*(g->x);   /* compute X,Y center */
  int y = 240-2*(g->y);
  int z = 30+(g->z);      /* size prop. to Z */

  rectangle(x-z,y-z,x+z,y+z);
 }


 int xx = 0;               /* plot position */

 drawp(glove_data *g)    /* plot X,Y data to test smoothing */
 {
  if(g->keys==4)    /* restart at left edge if "4" pressed */
```

```
   {
    cleardevice();
    xx=0;
   }

  setcolor(0);
  line(xx,0,xx,479);
  line(xx+1,0,xx+1,479);
  setcolor(15);
  line(xx,240-2*g->x,xx+1,240-2*g->x);
  setcolor(12);
  line(xx+1,240-2*g->y,xx+2,240-2*g->y);
  xx++;
  xx++;
  if(xx>639)xx=0;
 }


 int ox = -1000;                /* last x,y for hysterisis */
 int oy = -1000;

 dehyst(glove_data *g)          /* hysterisis deglitch (low noise removal) */
 {
  int x = g->x;
  int y = g->y;

  if(g->keys==0) ox = oy = 0;   /* handle recentering ("O"key or "Center") */

  if(x-ox>XHYST) ox = x-XHYST; /* X hysterisis */
  if(ox-x>XHYST) ox = x+XHYST;

  if(y-oy>YHYST) oy = y-YHYST; /* Y hysterisis */
  if(oy-y>YHYST) oy = y+YHYST;

  g->x = ox;                /* replace present X,Y data */
  g->y = oy;
 }


 int x1 = 0;                /* delayed 1 sample (for smoothed velocity test) */
 int y1 = 0;
 int x2 = 0;                /* delayed 2 samples */
 int y2 = 0;
 int lx = 0;                /* last good X,Y speed */
 int ly = 0;
 int lax = 0;               /* bad data "stretch" counter */
 int lay = 0;
 int lsx = 0;               /* X,Y "hold" values to replace bad data */
 int lsy = 0;
 int lcx = 0;               /* last X,Y speed for accel. calc. */
 int lcy = 0;
```

```
deglitch(glove_data *g)
{
 int vx, vy;

 int x = g->x;
 int y = g->y;

 if(g->keys==0)          /* reset on recentering ("0" or "Center" key) */
  {
   x1 = x2 = y1 = y2 = 0;
   lx = ly = lax = lay = 0;
   lsx = lsy = lcx = lcy = 0;
  }

 vx = x-((x1+x2)>>1);    /* smoothed velocity */
 vy = y-((y1+y2)>>1);

 x2 = x1;               /* update last values */
 x1 = g->x;

 y2 = y1;
 y1 = g->y;

 if(abs(lcx-vx)>XACC) lax = XXTEND;  /* check for extreme acceleration */
 if (lax == 0) lx=vx;    /* save only good velocity */
 lcx = vx;          /* save velocity for next accel. */

 if(abs(lcy-vy)>YACC) lay = YXTEND;  /* same deal for Y accel. */
 if (lay == 0) ly=vy;
 lcy = vy;

 if(lax!=0)       /* hold X pos'n if glitch */
  {
   g->x = lsx;
   lax--;
  }

 if(lay!=0)       /* hold Y pos'n if glitch */
  {
   lay--;
   g->y = lsy;
  }

 lsx = g->x;       /* save position for X,Y hold */
 lsy = g->y;


/* g->y = x;*/
}
```

Credits for the above go to the following individuals:

- Chris Babcock (72657,2126)

- John Eagan (76130,2225), Section leader, Virtual Reality section of CompuServe Computer Art forum

- Originally "power.c" (c) manfredo 9/91 (manfredo@opal.cs.tu-berlin.de)

- Developed on an ATARI 1040ST with TC 1.1 using a logic analyzer to get the correct timings

- Ported to PC compatibles by Greg Alt 10/91 (galt@peruvian.utah.edu or galt@es.dsd.com).

- Substantially rewritten by Dave Stampe (c) 1991: PWRFILT.C (dstamp@watserv1.uwaterloo.ca); 17/10/91

Index

About the Author

Nicholas Lavroff spent his early childhood in Cairo, Egypt (where he was born) and his formative years in Sydney, Australia. A graduate of the University of Sydney (where he obtained a Ph.D in psychology) and of Hastings College of the Law, Mr. Lavroff has spent the last twenty years living and working in San Francisco. Among his various occupations he lists cab driver, gardener, salesman, lawyer, and more recently, computer writer and consultant. He feels that all these experiences have provided him with some measure of depth, even without the use of 3D glasses.

In 1983 Mr. Lavroff sidestepped a budding law career to pursue a lifelong interest in technology. Since then he has written more than a dozen user manuals for commercial software products, and more than thirty articles and product reviews for national computer magazines. As a producer with software publisher Electronic Arts, he was responsible for several critically acclaimed products, including the MS-DOS version of DeluxePaint II, and Studio/8 for the Macintosh. More recently, he designed and produced Sargon V, the next-generation computer chess program for MS-DOS computers.

Mr. Lavroff lives with his wife, Cathy, and their cat, Benny, in San Francisco's Noe Valley.

Books have a substantial influence on the destruction of the forests of the Earth. For example, it takes 17 trees to produce one ton of paper. A first printing of 30,000 copies of a typical 480 page book consumes 108,000 pounds of paper which will require 918 trees!

Waite Group Press™ is against the clear-cutting of forests and supports re-forestation of the Pacific Northwest of the United States and canada, where most of this paper comes from. As a publisher with several hundred thousand books sold each year, we feel an obligation to give back to the planet. We will therefore support and contribute a percentage of our proceeds to organizations which seek to preserve the forests of planet Earth.

Can You See N.E. THING?

If you have overcome the widespread belief that seeing is believing, then you are ready for **N.E. THING!** We have taken care to create products that will give you second thoughts about one of your five senses and some serious insight into perceptions you might have taken for granted.

You <u>can</u> join the gaze craze!

For free information and more examples, please write to us at:

N.E. THING Enterprises, P.O. Box 1827, Cambridge, MA 02139.

*To see the image above, diverge your eyes, as if looking at a faraway object. The two dots will fuse, forming a third central dot. When the divergence is correct, slight, controlled variations in the placement of the random dots are perceived by the brain as depth cues. A shape will appear to float above a textured background. Some see the image in seconds. Others find it more difficult. If you can t see it, let someone else try. If they succeed, perhaps they can help you. Be sure to get the full explanation and more examples by writing for free information!

FRACTAL CREATIONS

Explore the Magic of Fractals on Your PC

by Timothy Wegner and Mark Peterson

Over 40,000 computer enthusiasts who've purchased this book/software package are creating and exploring the fascinating world of fractals on their computers. **Fractal Creations** includes a full color fractal art poster, 3-D glasses, and *Fractint*, the revolutionary software that makes fractals accessible to anyone with a PC. *Fractint* lets you zoom in on any part of a fractal image, rotate it, do color-cycle animation, and even choose accompanying sound effects and a 3-D mode. PC Magazine said "**Fractal Creations**…is a magical ride…guaranteed to blow your eyes out." Winner of the 1991 Computer Press Association Award for "Best Non-Fiction Computer Book." For MS/PC DOS machines; best with a VGA video board and a 286/386 processor.

ISBN 1-878739-05-0, 315 pp., 1 5.25" disk, color poster, 3-D glasses, $34.95 US/$44.95 Can., Available now

IMAGE LAB

Explore, Manipulate, and Create Images on Your PC

by Tim Wegner

Image Lab is a complete IBM PC-based "digital darkroom" in a unique book/disk package that covers virtually all areas of graphic processing and manipulation, and comes with the finest graphics shareware available today: *PICLAB, CSHOW, IMPROCES, Image Alchemy,* and others. The software included in Image Lab lets you size images, remove colors, adjust palettes, combine, crop, transform, ray trace, convert from one graphics file format to another, and render your images. Graphics expert Tim Wegner shows how to make 3-D fractals and combine them to make photorealistic scenes. The powerful *POV-Ray* program and clever examples are worth the price of the book alone. Full color stereo glasses are available along with detailed directions for making your own stereoscopic full color images. Best on MS/PC DOS 386 machines with a VGA video board.

ISBN 1-878739-11-5, 350 pp., 1 HD 3.5" disk, color poster, $39.95 US/$49.95 Can., Available August 1992

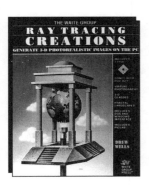

RAY TRACING CREATIONS

Create 3-D Photorealistic Images on the PC

by Drew Wells

With the **Ray Tracing Creations** book/disk combination, you can immediately begin rendering perfect graphic objects like the ones in computer movies. Using the bundled powerful shareware *POV-Ray* program, you'll learn to control the location, shape, light, shading, and surface texture of all kinds of 3-D objects. *POV-Ray's* C-like language is used to describe simple objects, planes, spheres, and more complex polygons. Over 100 incredible pre-built scenes are included that can be generated, studied, and modified any way you choose. This book provides a complete course in the fundamentals of ray tracing that will challenge and entice you. Contains 386 and 286 versions of *POV-Ray*; VGA display required. For MS/PC DOS machines.

ISBN 1-878739-27-1, 400 pp., 1 HD 3.5" disk, 3-D glasses, $39.95 US/$49.95 Can., Available December 1992

Send for our unique catalog to get more information about these books, as well as our outstanding and award-winning programming titles, including:

Master C: Let the PC Teach You C and **Master C++:** Let the PC Teach You Object-Oriented Programming. Both are book/disk software packages that turn your computer into an infinitely patient C and C++ professor.

Workout C: Hundreds of C projects and exercises and a full-featured C compiler make this an unbeatable training program and value.

C++ Primer Plus: Written by Stephen Prata in the same style as his C Primer Plus, which won the Computer Press Association's coveted "Best How-To Computer Book" award and sold over 400,000 copies.

Object Oriented Programming in Turbo C++: Robert Lafore, master teacher of the programming art, takes the prospective C++ programmer from the basics

to the most complex concepts, and provides anyone with C++ programming experience a comprehensive reference.

Windows API Bible: The only comprehensive guide to the 800 instructions and messages in the Windows Application Programming Interface.

Visual Basic How-To and **Visual Basic Super Bible.** Both books cover the unique Microsoft language that makes Windows programming much more accessible. **How-To** covers tricks, tips, and traps of VB programming. **Super Bible** is the ultimate compendium of reference information on VB.

Turbo Pascal How-To: Everything you need to know to begin writing professional Turbo Pascal programs.

MULTIMEDIA CREATIONS
Hands-On Workshop for Exploring Animation
by Philip Shaddock

Contemplating the jump into multimedia? Do it with **Multimedia Creations** and its powerful bundled *GRASP* program. Whether novice or programmer, you can create your own animated interactive audio-visual programs: from concept through post production, renderings to video tape. After a brief primer on PC video systems and animation fundamentals, you can start working with *GRASP*, creating everything from educational programs to your own multimedia cartoons. Work through the entire book/disk package to learn tricks like windowing, color cycling, sprite animation, delta compression techniques, and classical flipbook-style animation. And there are advanced chapters with in-depth coverage and reference sources for power users. Accompanying shareware programs provide you with the basic tools for creating complete multimedia presentations on the PC. For MS/PC DOS machines.

ISBN 1-878739-26-3, 450 pp, 2 5.25" disks, $44.95 US/$56.95 Can., Available October 1992

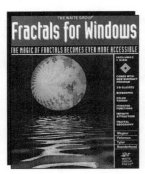

FRACTALS FOR WINDOWS
The Magic of Fractals Becomes Even More Accessible
by Tim Wegner, Mark Peterson, Bert Tyler, and Pieter Branderhorst

This is a perfect companion to **Fractal Creations**, but it probes deeper. It is bundled with *WINFRACT*, a powerful Windows program which enables you to play with over 80 fractals, or create totally new fractals, controlling your experiments simply with a zoom box, buttons, dialog boxes, menus, and a mouse. And because *WINFRACT*'s core technology is the latest version 18 of *FRACTINT* for DOS, it's faster than lightning at computing fractals. Plus you can generate fractals in the background! If you don't have any programming experience, that's ok. We've designed this package so you can still climb on board. But if you are a programmer, you'll love this rich resource of spectacular images you can use with other Windows programs.

ISBN 1-878739-25-5, 350 pp, 1 HD 3.5" disk, color poster, 3-D glasses,
$34.95 US/$44.95 Can., Available December 1992

TO ORDER TOLL FREE CALL 1-800-368-9369
TELEPHONE 415-924-2575 • FAX 415-924-2576

SEND ORDER FORM BELOW TO: WAITE GROUP PRESS, 200 TAMAL PLAZA, CORTE MADERA, CA 94925

Qty	Book	US/Can Price	Total
____	C++ Primer Plus	$26.95/34.95	_____
____	Fractal Creations ☐ 3.5" ☐ 5.25" disk	$34.95/44.95	_____
____	Fractals For Windows	$34.95/44.95	_____
____	Image Lab	$39.95/49.95	_____
____	Master C ☐ 3.5" ☐ 5.25" disks	$44.95/56.95	_____
____	Master C++ ☐ 3.5" ☐ 5.25" disks	$39.95/49.95	_____
____	Multimedia Creations	$44.95/56.95	_____
____	OOP in Turbo C++	$29.95/32.95	_____
____	Ray Tracing Creations	$39.95/49.95	_____
____	Turbo Pascal How-To	$24.95/32.95	_____
____	Visual Basic How-To	$34.95/44.95	_____
____	Visual Basic Super Bible	$39.95/49.95	_____
____	Windows API Bible	$39.95/49.95	_____
____	Workout C	$39.95/49.95	_____

Calif. residents add 7.25% Sales Tax _____

Shipping
UPS ($5 first book/$1 each add'l) _____
UPS Two Day ($10/$2) _____
Canada ($10/$4) _____

TOTAL _____

Ship to

Name _____

Company _____

Address _____

City, State, Zip _____

Phone _____

Payment Method
☐ Check Enclosed   ☐ VISA   ☐ MasterCard

Card# _____ Exp. Date _____

Signature _____

SATISFACTION GUARANTEED
OR YOUR MONEY BACK.
NO QUESTIONS ASKED.

SUPERSCAPE®
Virtual Realities

Desktop VR™
Turnkey Visualisation System

Virtual Reality Toolkit™
Interactive Virtual World Creation

For a FREE Information Pack on the complete
Dimension International product range, please contact:-

Zephyr One, Calleva Park, Aldermaston, Berkshire, England, RG7 4QZ
Tel: +44 (0)734 810077 Fax: +44 (0)734 816940

Please fill out this card if you wish to know of future updates to
Virtual Reality Playhouse, or to receive our catalog.

Satisfaction Report Card

Company Name:

Division: _____ Mail Stop:

Last Name: _____ First Name: _____ Middle Initial:

Street Address:

City: _____ State: _____ Zip:

Daytime telephone: (   )

Date product was acquired: Month _____ Day _____ Year _____ Your Occupation:

Overall, how would you rate _Virtual Reality Playhouse?_
☐ Excellent   ☐ Very Good   ☐ Good
☐ Fair   ☐ Below Average   ☐ Poor

What did you like MOST about this product? _____

_____

What did you like LEAST about this product? _____

_____

How do you use this book (entertainment, education, etc.)?

_____

Did you enjoy the approach of this book?

_____

What is your level of computer expertise?
☐ New   ☐ Dabbler   ☐ Hacker
☐ Power User   ☐ Programmer   ☐ Experienced professional

What is the primary use for your PC??

_____

Please describe your computer hardware:
Computer _____   Hard disk _____
5.25" disk drives _____   3.5" disk drives _____
Video card _____   Monitor _____
Printer _____   Peripherals _____

Where did you buy this book?
☐ Bookstore (name: _____)
☐ Discount store (name: _____)
☐ Computer store (name: _____)
☐ Catalog (name: _____)
☐ Direct from WGP
☐ Other

What price did you pay for this book? _____

What influenced your purchase of this book?
☐ Recommendation   ☐ Advertisement
☐ Magazine review   ☐ Store display
☐ Mailing   ☐ Book's format
☐ Reputation of The Waite Group   ☐ Topic

How many computer books do you buy each year? _____

How many other Waite Group books do you own? _____

What is your favorite Waite Group book?

_____

Is there any subject you would like to see The Waite Group cover in a similar approach?

_____

Additional comments? _____

_____

☐ **Check here for a free Waite Group Press™ catalog**